A First Course in Information Technology
Tutor's Manual

Leslie Cowan   Jane Higgins

Oxford University Press 1988

Oxford University Press, Walton Street, Oxford OX2 6DP

Oxford New York Toronto
Delhi Bombay Calcutta Madras Karachi
Petaling Jaya Singapore Hong Kong Tokyo
Nairobi Dar es Salaam Cape Town
Melbourne Auckland

and associated companies in
Berlin Ibadan

Oxford is a trade mark of Oxford University Press

© J. Cowan and J Higgins 1900

ISBN 019 832749 8

Typeset by Infotype, Eynsham
and printed in Great Britain by
the Alden Press, Oxford

Contents

1	About the Tutor's Manual	5
2	Introduction to computer systems	8

Transparency references
2.1 Manual and computer-based information processing systems — 11
2.2 Data representation and storage — 12
2.3 Formatting. Retrieval of data — 13
2.4 Other forms of data input — 15

3 Processing and output — 37

The BIRTHDAY.BAS program — 41

Transparency references
3.1 Basic principles for instructing a computer — 45
3.2 Flowchart to illustrate the algorithm for deleting a specified record from file — 46
3.3 Matrix and daisywheel principles — 47

4 First steps in database design and use — 59

Worksheet — 60

Transparency references
4.1 Program-centred and data-centred information systems and simple definition of a database — 63
4.2 The nature of data – quantitative and qualitative — 64
4.3 Obtaining information from data. Definitions of fields and records — 64

5 First steps in wordprocessing — 84

Worksheet — 88

Transparency references
5.1 Text enhancement and font choices — 93
5.2 Boilerplating — 93
5.3 Mailshots — 94
5.4 Text formatting — 94
5.5 Ergonomic considerations — 94
5.6 Disk catalogues — 95
5.7 Print positions, pitch and paper sizes — 96
5.8 Widows and orphans — 96

6 First steps in spreadsheet design and use — 117

Worksheet — 123

Transparency references
6.1 Introduction to spreadsheet concepts — 127
6.2 Spreadsheet grid — 127
6.3 Illustrations of valid and invalid ranges — 127
6.4 Spreadsheet applications — 128

7 Communications on computer systems — 139

Transparency references
7.1 Introduction to Wide Area Networks — 140
7.2 The Open Systems Interconnection (OSI) model — 141
7.3 Wide and Local Area Networks; network topology — 143
7.4 Local Area Networks — 145

8 Applications software — 159

Worksheet — 168

Transparency references
8.1 Input data controls — 171

Appendix 1 — 176

Transparency references
FS1 Disk handling — 176
FS2 Systems-related transparencies — 176
FS3 Check digits — 179

Appendix 2 — 201

I ASCII character codes — 201
II Word processing exercise 1 — 202
III Word processing exercise 2 — 204
IV Conversion grid for calculating line and character positions — 206
V P11 tax form — 207

Acknowledgements

The publishers would like to thank the Controller of Her Majesty's Stationery Office for granting permission to reproduce the P11 tax form: p. 207/208.

CHAPTER 1 | About the Tutor's Manual

This book is intended for the use of tutors whose students are using the book *A First Course in Information Technology*.

The Student's Book includes a number of student-based assignments and, as far as is possible in a volume which emphasizes basic principles rather than instructions for particular software or hardware, we have encouraged students to be self-sufficient. But there are inevitably going to be times when students will want to turn to someone who has walked the path before and can guide them over the difficult patches. This volume will supply material which will be helpful to those in the tutor's role.

In many cases, the students will be in the 16–19 age range and the tutor, a Sixth Form teacher or a college lecturer. In other cases, the student will be older, following the text for a better understanding of the use of computers in a business environment. Then, it may be a more senior person in the same office who becomes the tutor. Such a person will have quite a different approach from the tutor with a group of 15 or more students, but we are attempting in this manual to provide something useful for both.

Perhaps at the outset we should make the point that Information Technology can be an excellent integrating study if you wish to use it that way. It demands and encourages literacy and numeracy, and it develops habits of accuracy and a disciplined approach to work. With suitable tutorial support, students improve their investigative skills and powers of comprehension.

So, in terms of developing core skills, personal skills and specific skills both in IT and in vocational fields such as accounting, the book has much to offer. If teachers are able to offer students a range of different machines to work on (even if they are all IBM compatible) it helps them to see that their skills are transferable.

It is, of course, possible to take a much narrower, strictly IT, approach and it may be appropriate to do so for some students; the breadth of approach is a matter for the tutor's judgement. However, we feel bound to point out the great opportunities offered for enhancing student skills outside the strict confines of IT.

As we have indicated already, the book is designed to encourage individual learning through practical assignments. More and more emphasis is being placed on this approach which, over many years, has been proved effective. BTEC, for example, looks towards about half of any course material being learned in this way.

We accept that individual learning is not easy to manage, when there is only one tutor looking after a group of, say, 20 students.

There is, however, scope for some group work and we have provided additional examples and material not mentioned in the student text, in this manual, which can be used for group teaching sessions. At the end of each chapter we have included transparency masters, from which you may make your own foils. We have also included a few masters which can be photocopied for handouts and some material which may be helpful to students wishing to assess the extent of their learning for a particular topic. Such student work could, if subject to tutorial review, make a useful contribution to the student's personal notes.

There are some transparency suggestions which are not all chapter-specific; for example those covering systems aspects, whilst perhaps more closely associated with Chapters 2 and 3 than others, are nevertheless likely to be used in other contexts. Such transparencies we have described as 'free-standing' and they appear in groups in Appendix 1.

Just a brief word about the use of our transparency masters. You are welcome to copy them, but straight copying will in general produce monochrome teaching aids which can be a little uninteresting, and in some cases the use of colour is almost an essential to the understanding of the idea being conveyed. This is often so when overlays are being used: for example when a range of input and output devices are associated with a processor early in Chapter 2. Here, as in all cases where overlays are used, a separate master sheet has been provided for each sheet of the overlay, and if you have access to a small desk-top copier with cartridge inserts containing toner, you could use different toner colours for each of the three transparencies involved, thus reinforcing the distinct areas of *input – processing – output*.

Multicolour single transparencies could be produced on the same equipment by masking part of the master whilst making a transparency copy of the unmasked parts in one colour, then changing the masking and the cartridge colour before passing the same transparency through the machine again. However, if you decide to use the masters as source material, you may prefer simply to extract certain ideas and originate your own transparencies.

A number of the transparencies are best suited to presentation by a progressive revelation technique, but these will be obvious to teachers and lecturers and no guidance is offered on the subject of presentation, other than to make it clear where a group of master sheets are to be used together as overlays.

The notes preceding the transparency masters for each chapter act as a brief commentary. In no way are they intended to be prescriptive, but in our experience, other people's visuals are of little value if one has no idea of the context in which the originator intended them to be presented. In these notes, the transparency masters are referred to by number, and this number will be found printed in the top left-hand or top right-hand corner of each sheet.

The extent to which software provides useful on-screen help varies quite considerably, and there will be many occasions when students would like to look at the software handbooks. This may well introduce practical difficulties, as you may have only a few copies available, but that aside, even the better handbooks are often not well-organized from a learning point of view, and students have to know fairly precisely what they are looking for before they can begin to find it.

To help overcome this problem, we have included in some chapters *pro formas* which you can complete for the software available to your students, and then photocopy. The same form has been completed for one or two software packages which are popular and which you may be using. They cover many of the facilities available, but we have omitted the very obvious ones and have tried to restrict attention to commands which are likely to be used at an introductory level.

Finally, in this brief introduction, let us touch on the subject of equipment. If you are working in a school or college environment, the chances are that you will be using a network of microcomputers with software being called down from a shared hard disk and students' work being saved to other partitions on the same hard disk. You may only have one or two printers in the room.

However, in tens of thousands of businesses up and down the land, there are free-standing micros with built-in disk storage (two floppies, or more probably a hard disk and one floppy disk drive), memory of 512 Kbytes or more and possibly a 'go faster' card of some kind. Associated with the micro will be a printer.

Of course there are networks and multi-user systems in commercial use and there will be many more. But to equip students for the real world, we should certainly see that they can handle a free-standing system which includes at least one floppy disk drive. This is clearly the intention of the highly practical CGLI 726 Information Technology series, and from an educational standpoint, we think students learn much more from such a basic system than they do by coming to a network which is 'up and running'.

So, if you have a network, with perhaps the odd free-standing machine, we strongly recommend that students gain experience and some degree of competence in handling the free-standing system and its associated disks.

See to it that they get to handle all routine aspects of the printer too. The CGLI requires that students are capable of changing printer ribbons and daisywheels, loading stationery, etc. Fluency in such simple practical skills is essential in the business world.

At the very least a course based on the student text should produce a sufficient familiarity with both hardware and the software controlling it to remove any fear of handling computers and associated equipment. It should enable students to accept the use of computers as natural and commonplace, and it should provide an appreciation of applications which one might expect to use in the commercial world.

CHAPTER 2 Introduction to computer systems

The first few pages of this chapter in the student text are straightforward, but in them we develop the concept of a system as having basic components handling input, processing (with temporary local memory), longer term storage and output. In the initial discussion we limit ourselves with one input device – the keyboard – and two output devices – the VDU and a printer.

We think this is probably enough at this point, but the gaps, especially on the input side, are many and you may wish to fill some of them with some group work at an appropriate time. Transparency sequence 2.1 at the end of this chapter offers masters associated with this part of the work.

Perhaps the most common form of input, other than the keyboard, within the day-to-day experience of the student, is input by reading bar codes. Whilst we felt that exploring other forms of input and output was something which we could not give more space in the student text, it is an important topic. At the end of this chapter, in Appendix 1, we offer some transparency suggestions in Sequence 2.4 which may be helpful to you if you have enough time with the students to develop work on alternative input and output devices and techniques.

On bar codes, we go no further with these transparencies than illustrating the interleaved 2 in 5 code, although more complex codes are frequently used today. The 2 in 5 is a nice example of lateral thinking – moving away from the standard binary approach of 1, 2, 4, 8 to 1, 2, 4, 7 in order to accommodate parity checking, such that of five bars, two are always in the '1' state (thick) and three are in the '0' state (thin).

You could perhaps use the bar code transparencies effectively a week before using the transparencies in Sequence 2.2, which show the binary representation of characters, in which each byte comprises the 7-bit *ASCII* code and a parity bit. In this way, students would already be introduced to the concept of parity and this assignment will provide a foundation for what they will learn about the ASCII code itself.

But we are getting ahead of ourselves. Our immediate concern is the development of the concept of input – processing – output, and in the student text we suggest that the reader gives consideration to the check-out system at a supermarket. This analysis could well be handled in a group discussion; we would anticipate that the end result might look something like this:

Input 1: the goods which you place on the conveyor belt.

Processing: the production of a list of items or item codes and the corresponding prices; the maintenance of a running total.

Input 2: your £10 note.
Local memory: remembering the running total whilst the amount tendered is input and the change due calculated.
Further processing: calculation of the change due.
Output 1: your change.
Output 2: your goods.

It could be quite a lot more complex, depending on the ability level of your group. With a bright group, you may wish to introduce the concept of interrelated systems, with point-of-sale information being used to update both accounting and stock control systems.

As we begin to develop ideas for practical experimentation in Chapter 2 of the student text, the need for students to have access to a simple system which they can 'boot up' from a floppy system disk becomes apparent. (There is a free-standing Transparency sequence FS1, in Appendix 1 which relates to the care of floppy disks.) Only by handling a system in such a basic way, can the concept of reading in system files – and later, of using the external FORMAT command – be meaningful to students. By all means, let them boot from a hard disk or log on to a network if this is the normal practice; however they should also have experience of booting from a system floppy disk. When it comes to formatting, they should use the FORMAT command file on that disk, to format both the data disks and the disks to which the system transferred, so that they are working from first principles.

This raises another issue. There are suppliers of both networked and stand-alone systems, who make much of the fact that they bundle in front-end software such as GEM or WINDOWS. These products have their uses, but at introductory level, it is our view that they get in the way of a basic understanding of the system. They also take up memory space that could better be used for other things!

So if students under your guidance are using a system with an AUTOEXEC batch file which calls any kind of resident front-end software, we suggest that you either render the batch file ineffective as an AUTOEXEC, by changing its name, or at least modify it so that there is the opportunity for the user to work directly with the operating system.

Much of Chapter 2 is given over to the operating system and system basics; we invite the student to get as much practice as possible in the use of internal commands. These will enable the display of directories and facilitate the copying and deletion of files, both singly and in batches, determined by the use of *wild cards*.

You will want to exercise control over this, taking into account both the available hardware and the ability of your students. For example, if we assume twin floppy drives and a group of no more than average ability, we might restrict MSDOS copy commands by insisting (in relation to a twin disk system) that the file(s) to be copied are on the disk in drive A and that the system is logged to that drive. Then the command is of the form

    COPY (filespec) B:

We do not complicate the issue by undertaking the same copy whilst logged on to drive B, or by copying from B to A, whereas with an above-average group this work could be done to advantage. Such students could also change the file name on copying. It should perhaps be added that although such flexibility is worth acquiring, it is better in practice to have a set copying pattern (our preference is from drive A to drive B). By developing such a routine, one is less prone to make expensive errors when under pressure or getting tired.

You may well find that some students, having used a command once or twice will feel that is enough and want to press on with something else. But the basic system commands are of such importance that we feel they should be drilled until their use becomes virtually automatic.

In regard to the DIR command, some syllabuses call for a hard copy listing of the directory. We have not included this in the student text, but you may well wish to cover it with some students. One approach (with MSDOS) would be to use the CTRL P toggle to echo everything to printer, prior to typing the DIR command. Another approach would be to direct the screen output to the printer as one might to a file, because the system treats both console (the keyboard) and printer very much as it treats files. Thus a suitable command would be DIR >PRN, sending the directory output to the printer.

It would be early days with most students, but with a few, you might like to show the use of the pipe (|) to enable two commands to be handled by the system concurrently. In the present case, we would use DIR with SORT to provide a sorted directory list. If you do this, remember that not only must the file SORT.EXE be present on the logged drive, but the disk on which it is found must not be write-protected. This is because in operation the sort program needs to set up temporary files. An appropriate command could be

    DIR|SORT>PRN

These are just a few examples of the way you can extend the foundation work in the student text for selected individuals who can benefit from it.

FORMAT is the only external command which we expect all students to use when working through Chapter 2; we have already suggested SORT as a possible development of systems work for some students. Perhaps more generally, though, you may wish to introduce CHKDSK. This is an interesting utility for suitable students to investigate, because it not only gives the status of the disk, but also of the memory. It shows the amount of RAM occupied by the system (both hidden files and COMMAND.COM) and, of course, the CHKDSK program itself. But take care! With most systems the arithmetic may not work out the way you might expect. To quote a typical twin disk IBM compatible system:

    CHKDSK will show 262144 bytes total memory
                     237568 bytes free

from which you may deduce that the program CHKDSK and the system together are occupying 24576 bytes. (You will notice, by the way, that 262144 bytes is the same as 256 Kbytes, ie, 256 × 1024 [or 2^{10}]). Now CHKDSK also shows that the two hidden system files occupy 22528 bytes on the system disk and COMMAND.COM occupies 18016 bytes. So at face value, you might expect the system to occupy 40544 bytes when read into memory. In fact, it occupies less space, because some of the memory locations used when the earlier system files were read in, are reused by parts of the system which are read in subsequently. The degree of economy on memory space effected in this way, varies from one computer manufacturer to another, depending on exactly how they have implemented the operating system.

So if you do use CHKDSK as an extension to the limited work we cover in the student text on the use of external command files, be prepared to handle questions from your more inquisitive students as to why the arithmetic doesn't stack up.

We have already made specific references to three groups of transparencies associated with this chapter; the remaining one, Sequence 2.3 covers the concepts of formatting and retrieval of data from disk.

Transparencies dealing with system aspects have been included in Appendix 1 as the Sequence FS2. Certainly some of them would be appropriate for use at a very early stage; others you may wish to refer to much later. Since it seemed likely that this would be a sequence which you would dip into at various times, we felt it better to classify it as a free-standing sequence rather than belonging specifically to work in Chapter 2 or Chapter 3. However, we do think that considerable reference should be made to Sequence FS2 when students are working on Chapters 2 and 3.

Chapter 2 – Transparency sequence 1
A comparison between manual and computer-based information processing systems

Notes

Transparency reference

2.1.1 The objective here is first to consider any manual system and to distinguish the three component parts of *input – processing* (with use of local memory) – *output*; and then to show that a computer system parallels that real life situation.

Quite good group participation can be obtained by inviting students to suggest some totally different activity and then identify the several inputs, processes and outputs.

2.1.2a–c These three transparencies should be set up for use as overlays, and it is desirable for the sake of clarity to use a different colour for each transparency in the set.

We would emphasize that only *some* input and output devices are included (e.g. no mention of bar code readers, MICR or OCR input, etc.) but it is enough to meet immediate needs. See, however, Sequence 2.4 for some transparencies on some other input methods.

You may wish to point out that the disk is an I/O device.

Introduce the terms *modulation* (as the process for converting electrical signals from the form used by computers to a form suitable for transmission over the telephone system) and *demodulation* (as the converse); indicate that both processes are carried out by electronic circuitry in the same box and the equipment name – *modem* – is a conflation of *m*odulator/*dem*odulator.

There is sometimes confusion in students' minds about the classification of the screen solely as an output device; this arises from the fact that it usually echoes keyboard input so that the user can verify that the input is correct. But it is, of course, the keyboard which is the input device, and you may need to emphasize this.

2.1.3 Simply reinforces the input – processing – output concept and provides continuity. Group discussion at this point usually elicits such answers as 'It's faster'. Build on this and other appropriate replies to develop the essential features of any information system, based either on one or more of the activities arising from the discussion of Transparency sequence 2.1, or on a simple personnel card index file.

2.1.4, 2.1.5 2.1.4 summarizes the essential features of any information system, and needs to be followed up fairly quickly with 2.1.5. These two form the link between the first and second sequences. In the second sequence, *storage* is considered, and in later sequences some aspects of *retrieval*, *processing* and *output* are considered.

Chapter 2 – Transparency sequence 2
Concepts of data representation and storage

Reuse 2.1.4 and 2.1.5 simply to provide continuity from the first sequence and to present the second sequence, dealing with *storage*.

Notes

Transparency reference

2.2.1 This introduces the concept that an electromagnetic field can magnetize very small portions of the surface coating of a disk, and that the direction of polarity can be reversed. Although the '1' '0' symbolism is introduced, there is no reference on this transparency to *binary digit* or *bit*. The term should be introduced verbally at this point; it will be reinforced on the next transparency.

2.2.2 This transparency provides the opportunity to illustrate that each time another bit is added to the combination, the number of things which can be represented by the binary patterns is doubled. At this stage we ignore the fact that ASCII is in fact a 7-bit code with the eighth bit of the byte being used for parity checking. We use the simplifying assumption that a byte represents a character.

2.2.3 Partly reinforcement of points made in 2.2.1 and 2.2.2. The radial movement of the head is shown diagramatically and is best reinforced by reference to an actual 5¼ inch or disk.

This may be a timely point at which to discuss the handling and care of disks. This subject is treated in the Transparency sequence FS1, in Appendix 1, which can be used at any time.

2.2.4 The use of this transparency depends very much on the ability range of the group of students with whom you are working. In any event it introduces ASCII code and shows actual code for a few upper case and lower case letters and numbers 1–3. It also shows that the code itself is a 7-bit code and that the eighth bit is used for another purpose. You may find it helpful to use a distinctive colour for the data bits.

The need for international standards in coding and data communication can be touched on, because ASCII is a good example of a standard which has been adopted internationally.

For those students who can take it, the transparency can form the basis of teaching on:

1 Parity bits – why they are used and how they are used.
2 Some features of the code itself, e.g. the codes for upper and lower case of any alphabetic character differing only in the bit of weighting 32. This allows the teaching to be taken further into a preliminary discussion on pattern recognition as related to exact and hazy searches for a given string of characters.

If a hand-out showing ASCII codes is required, a photocopyable table of these can be found as item I, in Appendix 2.

2.2.5 This may be inappropriate for some student groups, but perhaps of use if specific ASCII codes are being referred to in denary terms. The purpose of the transparency is to help students count in binary and recognize that the columns have weightings of: units, 2, 2×2, 2×2×2, etc., in just the same way that the denary system has weightings of: units, 10, 10×10, 10×10×10, etc. The circles on the transparency represent '0' and they may be changed to '1's as counting proceeds, by placing 1p coins over the circles. (*Note*: you will need at least 15 of these.)

Although hexadecimal codes are also given in item I in Appendix 2, students will not need to know about Hex for some time (if at all). Therefore counting in and converting between number systems other than bases 2 and 10, is not pursued in this introductory text.

Chapter 2 – Transparency sequence 3
Formatting – what it is, why it is necessary. Retrieval of data

Notes

Transparency reference

2.3.1 Up to this point, the question of *how* data is coded and stored has been addressed, but not *where* it is stored (other than somewhere on the surface of a disk). The only point of storing data is that at some time we will want to recall and refer to it; so we (or rather the computer) must know exactly where it has been stored.

The map reference concept is useful in this context, and this transparency reproduces a section from a map in *The Oxford Practical Atlas* as an introductory foil. If you need reminding of map reading techniques, here's an example: the map reference of Stoke-on-Trent is 53°N2°15′W.

2.3.2 This transparency introduces the concept of tracks and sectors. The following points may be worth making:

1 The pattern of tracks and sectors is a *magnetic* pattern imprinted on the disks by a process called *formatting*.
2 There are no agreed standards for the number of tracks or sectors on a disk, so disks are sold blank (unformatted) and the user formats them for the kind of machine he is using. It follows that physically identical disks formatted for incompatible computer systems can only be used with the systems on which they were formatted.
3 *Tracks* are identifiable by radial position, *sectors* are identified by reference to the index hole. It is useful to have a 5¼ inch disk available at this point – preferably one where the jacket has been carefully split on one or more edges, so that the disk itself can be removed for inspection. Show the index hole and explain how a light source and receptor are used to provide an electrical pulse as the index hole passes the index window in the jacket.
4 Usually a sector contains 512 bytes on each track.
5 As users, we do not specify the track or sector where a particular block of data or program code is to be stored. The computer operating system does this for us and keeps a record of where it put it, so that we can get it back at a later date. (This is the first mention of operating systems.)

The transparencies in Sequence FS2 deal with operating systems in more detail.

2.3.3 The concept of directory tracks is introduced. This transparency is designed to be conceptual rather than realistic, in that it implies that files are held in 'blocks' on the disk, whereas in practice the sectors and tracks used for a single file are not contiguous. Points to be made:

1 A fixed space and position is always reserved on disk for the directory.
2 Because directory space is fixed, there is a limit to the number of files which may be held on a disk, even if the files are small and there is still plenty of room on the disk. Usually the limit is 112 files.
3 The directory contains for each file:
   i A file name which we give. (File names are covered by other transparencies.)
   ii The location of the track and sector where the operating system has placed the first part of the file.
   iii The file size (in bytes).
   iv The date and time at which the file was created or last amended. (More about date and time can be found under Operating Systems.)

2.3.4 With some students, it may be worth progressing to a brief discussion on interleaving techniques designed to improve reading speeds.

This transparency illustrates interleaving. The number of sectors skipped will depend on the disk speed and the computer clock speed. The objective is to have the next part of a stored file, which is spread over many sectors, passing under the read/write head at the earliest opportunity after the disk controller has dealt with the data read from a previous sector.

Chapter 2 – Transparency sequence 4
Other forms of data input

There are three very commonly found techniques used for direct data input to computer systems:

1 Techniques which rely on light transmission through parts of an opaque substance which has had holes punched in it. Punched paper tape and punched cards are obsolete examples of this, but Kimball tags are still in use in some major stores.
2 Techniques which rely on light reflection (or absence of reflection) as for example, Optical Mark data entry systems, or the reading of bar codes.
3 Magnetic pattern detection, where the characters may be humanly readable (as on cheques) or not (as in the magnetic strip on credit cards).

Of these three techniques, the first is best illustrated by laying actual Kimball tags on the OHP platten; the third is difficult to illustrate, and the transparencies in this sequence are confined to the second – the light reflective techniques.

Notes

Transparency reference

2.4.1 This illustrates two possible applications of Optical Mark cards. The second example shows specific data being marked.

2.4.2 to **2.4.5** The introduction of some bar code principles.

2.4.2 This transparency shows the coding patterns for the numerals 1–0 (*note* that 0 does not make numerical sense – its actual value would be 11 – but it does not follow the sequence through from 8 and 9).

2.4.3 This places a uniform gap between each bar, and should be used with an opaque overlay which has a slot cut out of it, just large enough to display the code for one figure at a time. Here we have added start and stop codes, and an illustration of the 2 in 5 bar code is given at the foot of this transparency.

2.4.4 The concept of interleaving is presented, and this is also an opportunity to make the point that each bar code system is identified by using different start/stop characters. It is perhaps worthwhile to overlay the bottom parts of 2.4.3 and 2.4.4 to show the saving of space achieved through interleaving.

2.4.5 An actual example of a commercial use of the 2 in 5 interleaved code, with an analysis of the code superimposed.

The Manual Processor and the Computer Processor

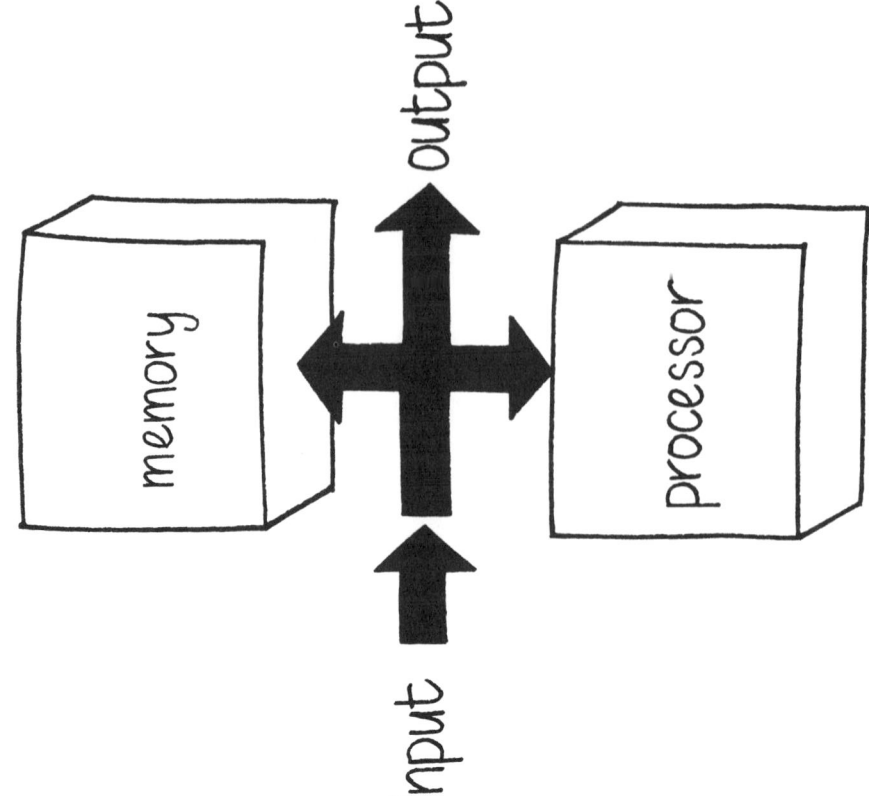

input...

keyboard

— disk

another
computer
(local)

telephone
line
modem
remote computer

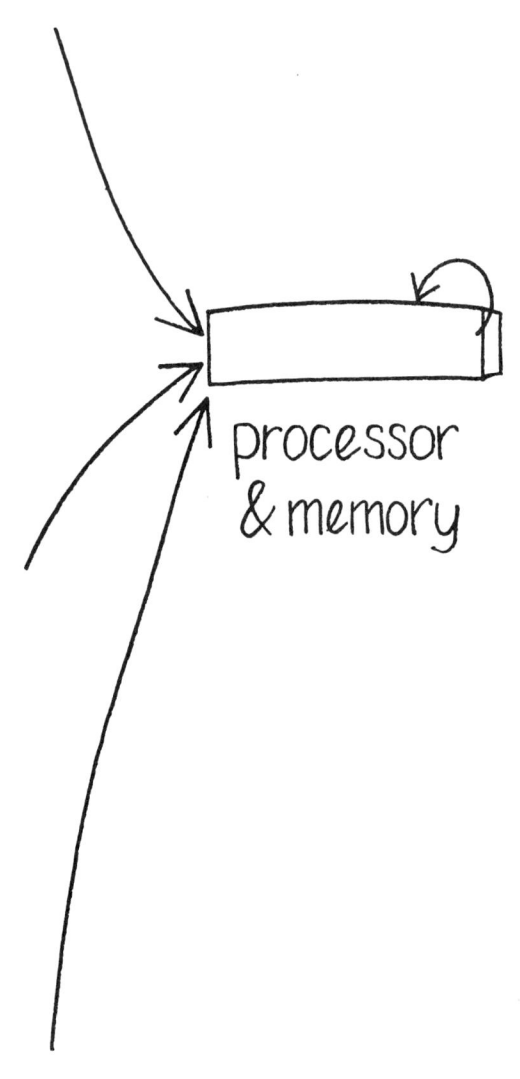

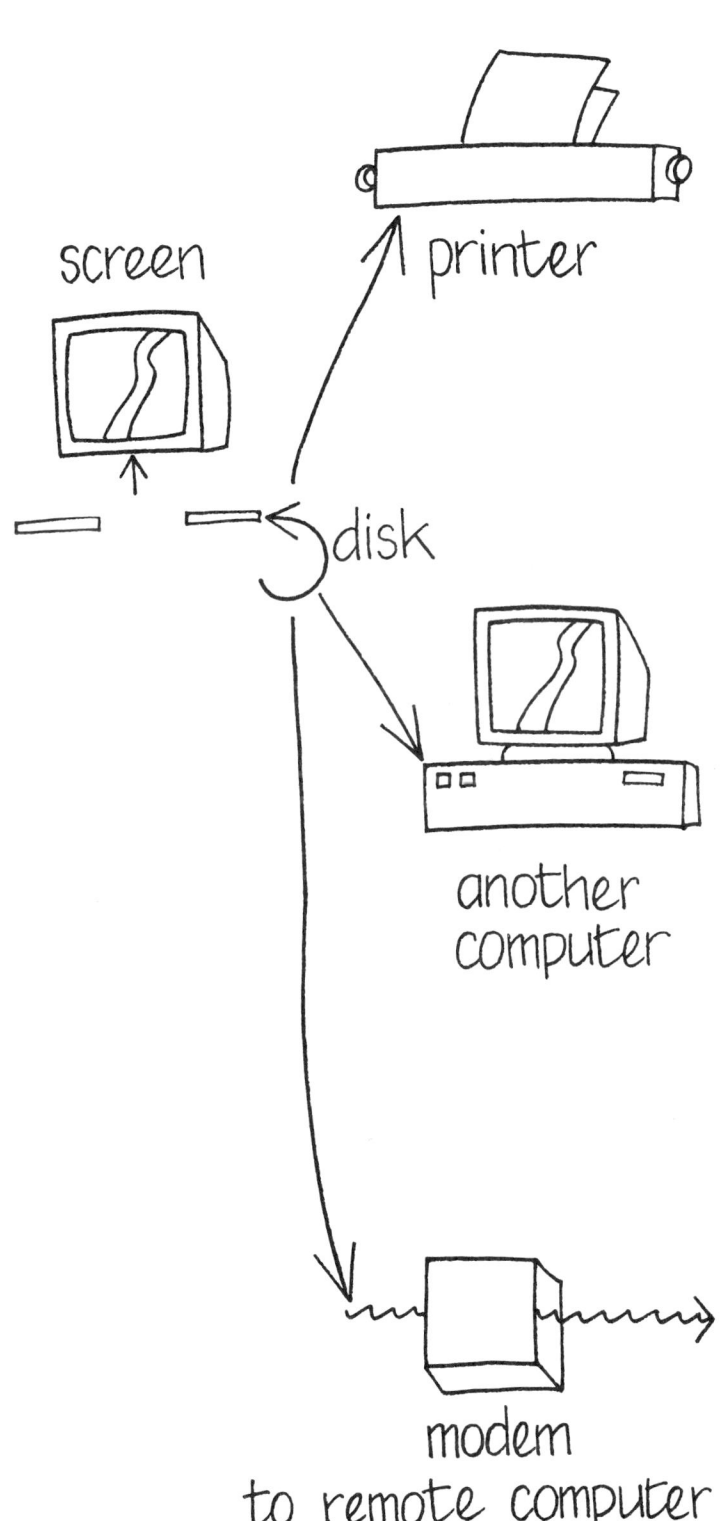

input . . .

processing . . . .
(using temporary
memory as necessary)

output . . .

. . . the same for a computer system
as for a manual system

SO WHY USE COMPUTERS?

Essential Features of an Information System

	data capture	from a live situation
	storage	of the data
subsequent	retrieval	of required data
	processing	of data in any of numerous ways
to produce	output	of information in required form

A computer is good at . . . .
storing data
    efficiently and compactly
retrieving data
    selectively and quickly
processing data
    sorting, selecting, counting and calculating at high speed
outputting information
    on screen or by hardcopy (printout) in any desired format
    and in any required location

Data Storage

Data storage is achieved by imprinting magnetic patterns on the disk surface.

This is done by the read/write head operating in 'write' mode, and magnetizing small particles of the disk surface

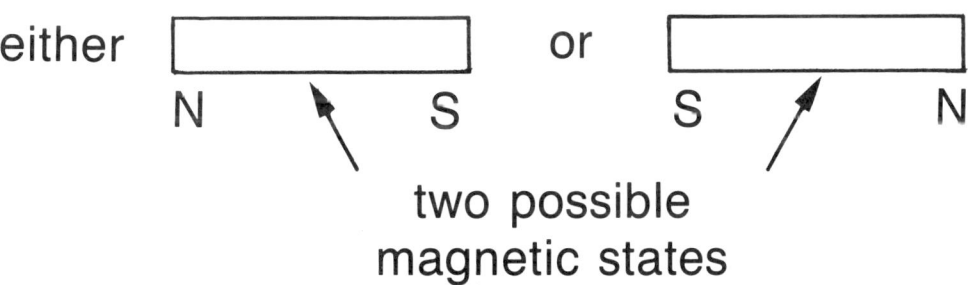

two possible magnetic states

Symbolically, we can refer to these as

'1' or '0'

Data Representation

A single binary digit (a **bit**) can only represent two things because it only has two states.

A combination of two bits allows representation of four different things:

```
0 0  =  first thing
0 1  =  second thing
1 0  =  third thing
1 1  =  fourth thing
```

Combining more bits allows the representation of more things. With 8 bits (called a **byte**) we can represent the characters A–Z, a–z, 0–9 plus punctuation, special characters and command symbols.

Writing to Disk

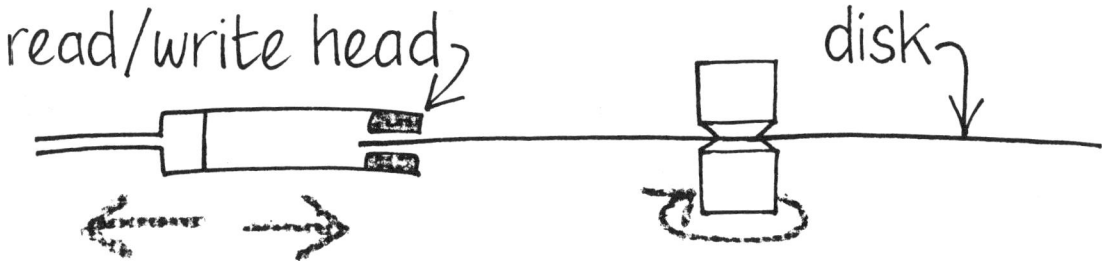

The write head imprints very small magnetic patterns on the disk surface.

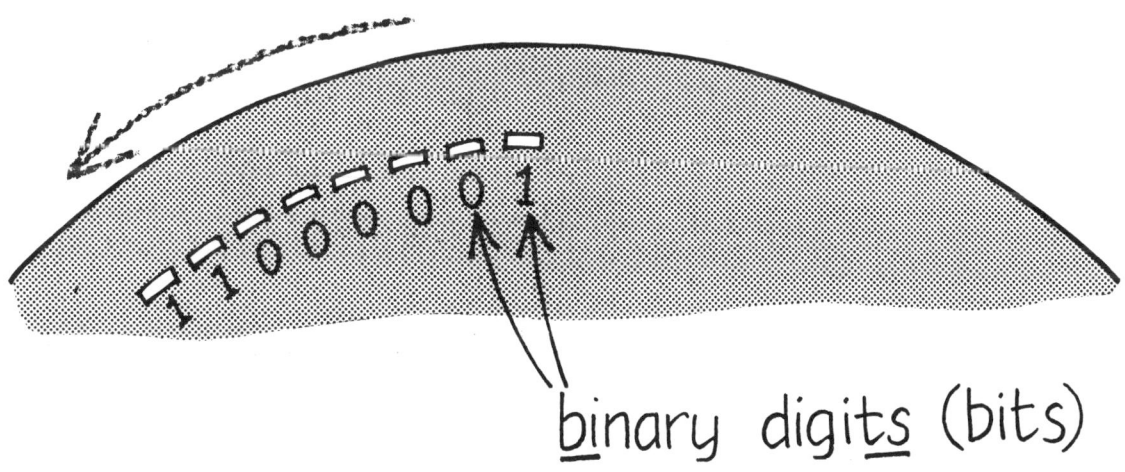

binary digits (bits)

8 bits = 1 byte (representing one character)

Example of ASCII Code

ASCII (the American Standard Code for Information Interchange) is a 7-bit code. The eighth bit of the byte may be used as a parity check digit. In this example, odd parity is assumed.

1	1	0	0	0	0	0	1	A
1	1	0	0	0	0	1	0	B
0	1	0	0	0	0	1	1	C
0	1	1	0	0	0	0	1	a
0	1	1	0	0	0	1	0	b
1	1	1	0	0	0	1	1	c
0	0	1	1	0	0	0	1	1
0	0	1	1	0	0	1	0	2
1	0	1	1	0	0	1	1	3

Counting in Binary

0

1

2

3

4

5

6

7

8

9

The Map Reference Analogy

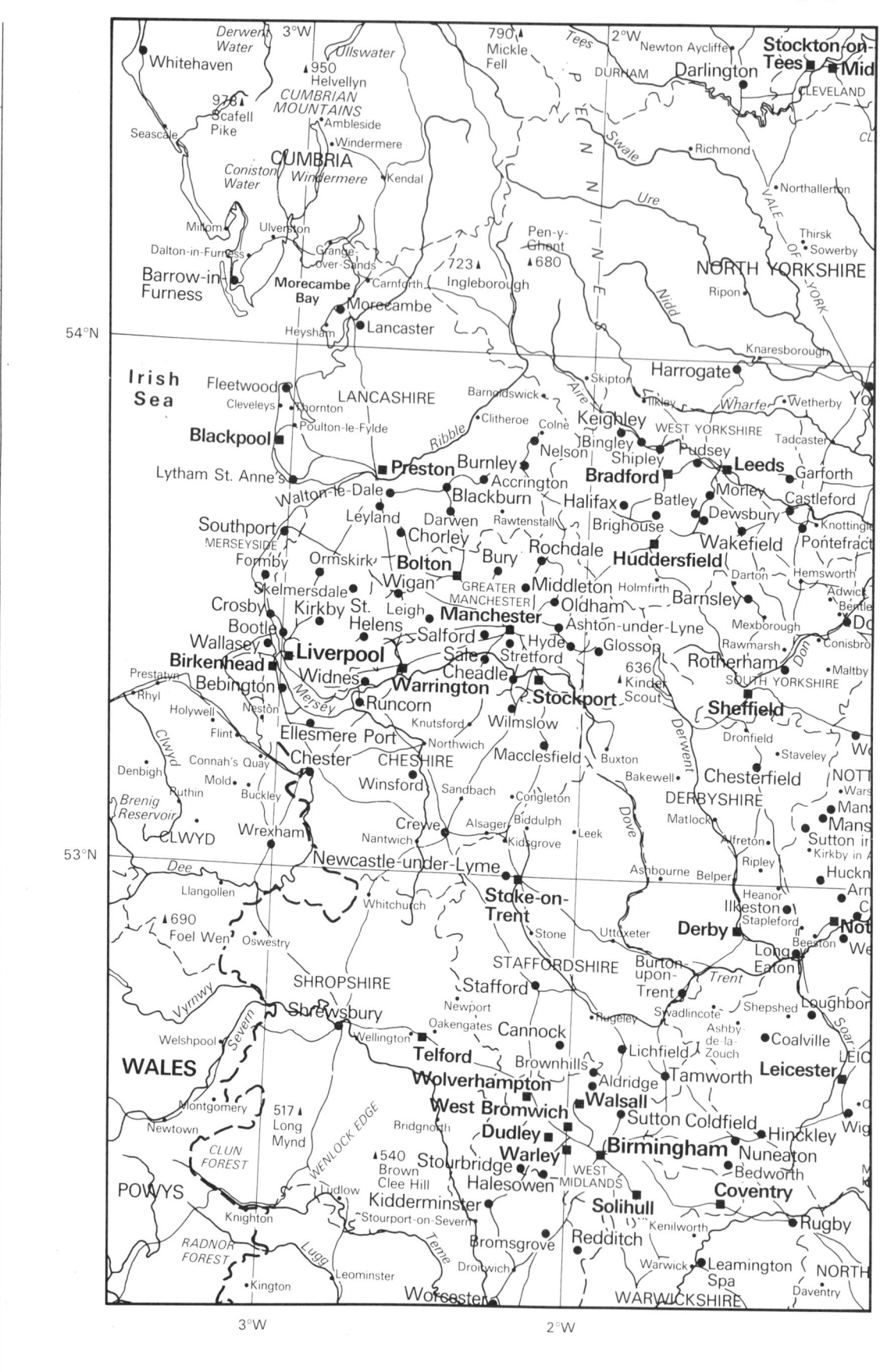

Disk Formatting

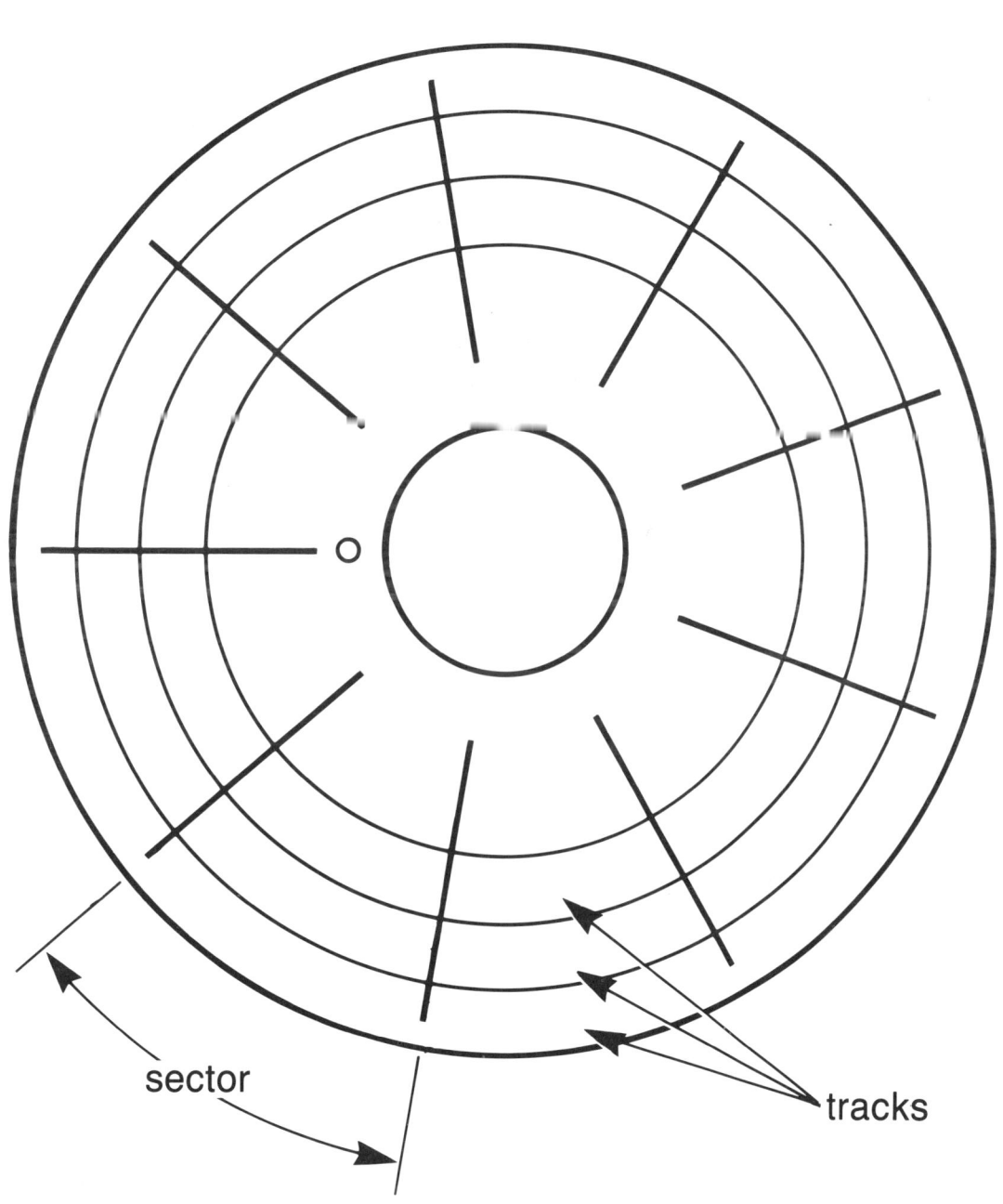

Disk Use by Computer

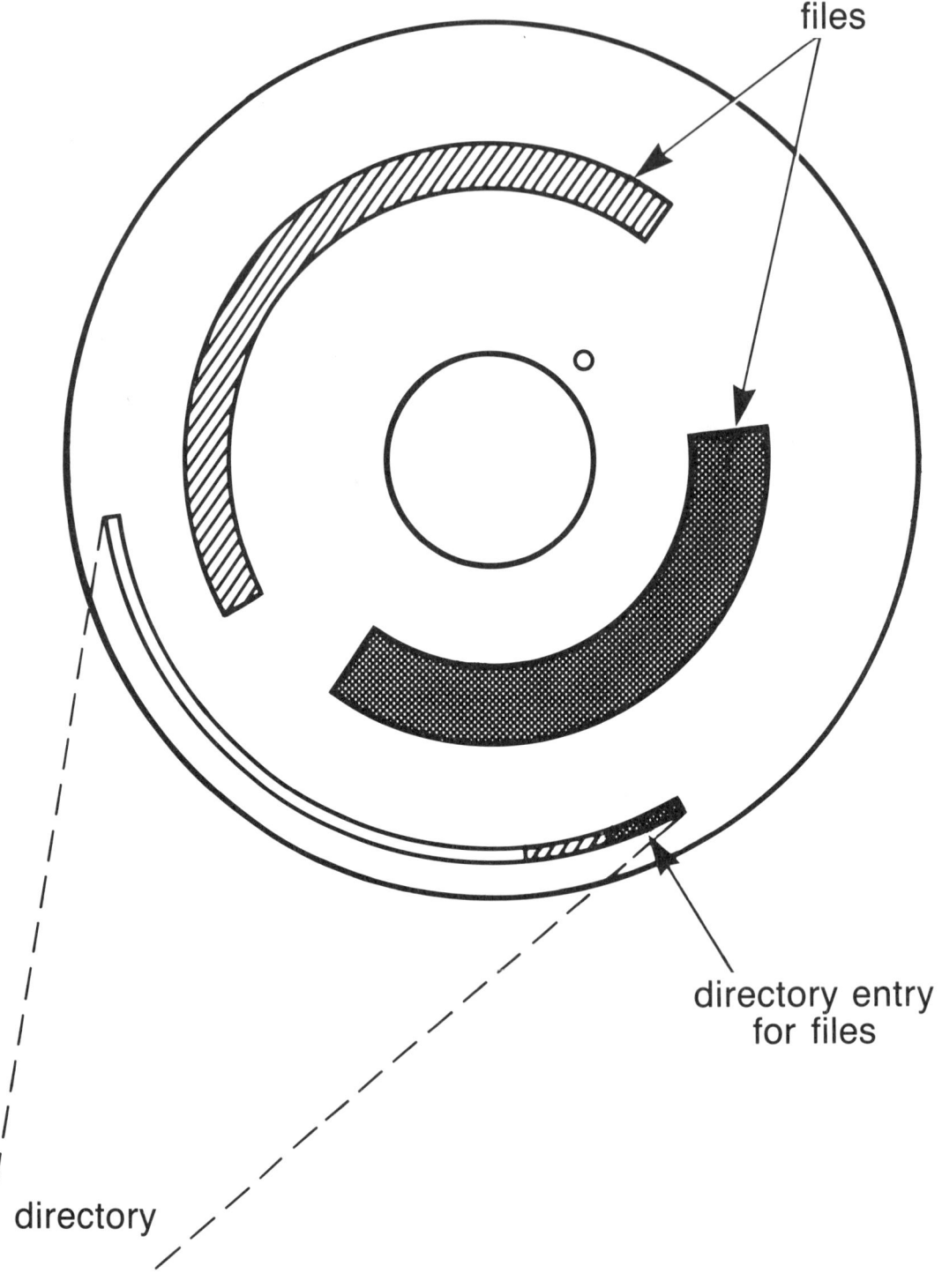

An Example of Interleaving

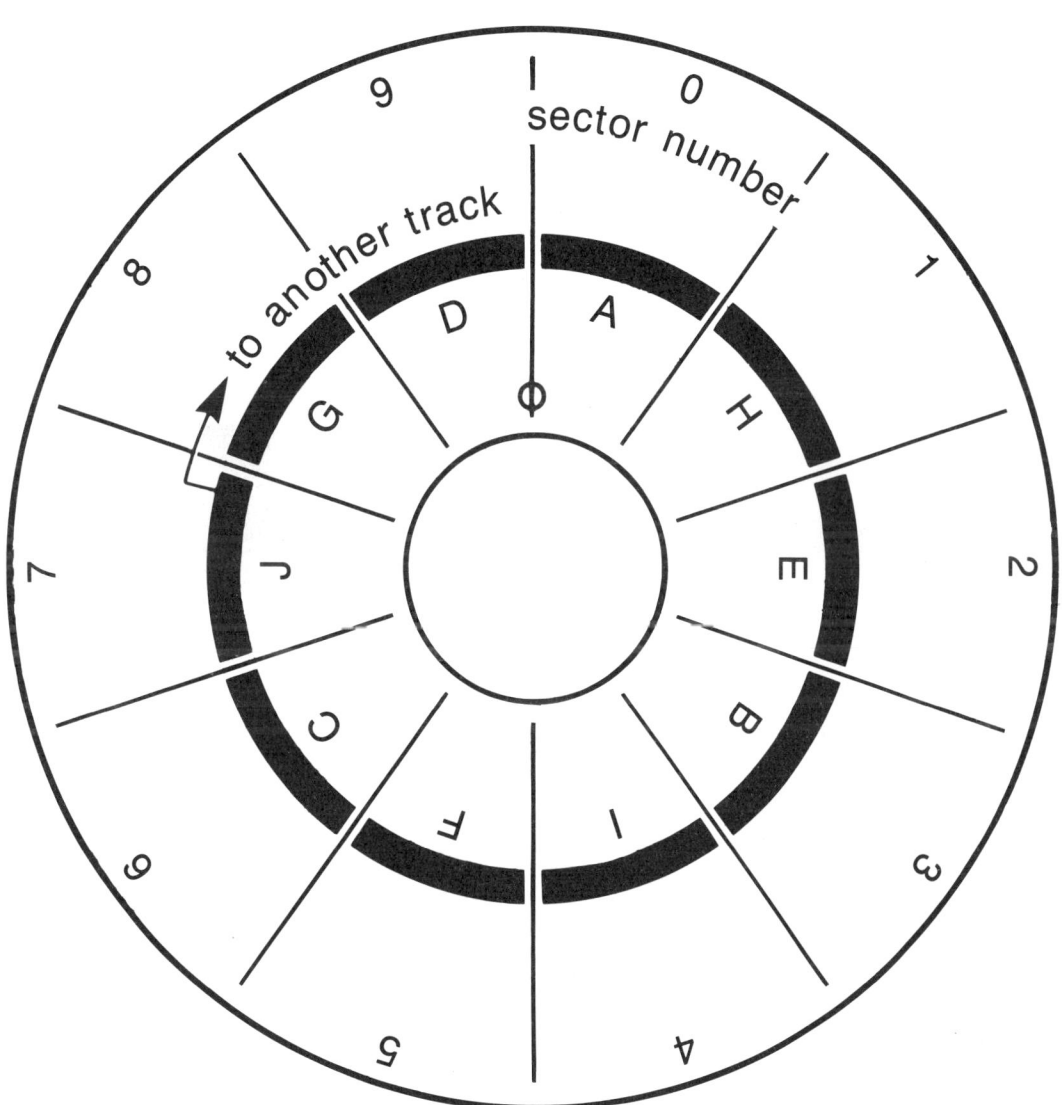

A–J are successive blocks of the same file

Examples of Optical Mark Data Entry

a Completion of Survey Material

How would you rate the listed aspects of your data entry system?					
	very good	good	satis-factory	poor	very poor
cost effectiveness	▭	▭	▭	▭	▭
speed of throughput	▭	▭	▭	▭	▭
overload capacity	▭	▭	▭	▭	▭
transcription accuracy	▭	▭	▭	▭	▭
input validation	▭	▭	▭	▭	▭
flexibility	▭	▭	▭	▭	▭

b Application involving alpha-numeric data

Employee No				Date of Birth		
				day	month	year
2	**7**	**3**	**4**	**31**	**July**	**66**
0	0	0	0	00	Jan	00
1	1	1	1	1̸	Feb	11
2̸	2	2	2	22	Mar	22
3	3	3̸	3	3̸3	Apl	33
4	4	4	4̸	4	May	44
5	5	5	5	5	Jun	55
6	6	6	6	6	J̸u̸l̸	6̸6̸
7	7̸	7	7	7	Aug	77

Bar Codes 1

Bar codes are based on a binary coded decimal representation of numbers. However, the weightings are 1,2,4,7 rather than 1,2,4,8, which allows a straight 2 of 5 coding.

2 in 5 coding uses 5 bars for each digit of which two are always wide and three narrow.

	1	2	4	7	PARITY
1	▮	▮	▮	▮	▮
2	▮	▮	▮	▮	▮
3	▮	▮	▮	▮	▮
4	▮	▮	▮	▮	▮
5	▮	▮	▮	▮	▮
6	▮	▮	▮	▮	▮
7	▮	▮	▮	▮	▮
8	▮	▮	▮	▮	▮
9	▮	▮	▮	▮	▮
0	▮	▮	▮	▮	▮

Bar Codes 2

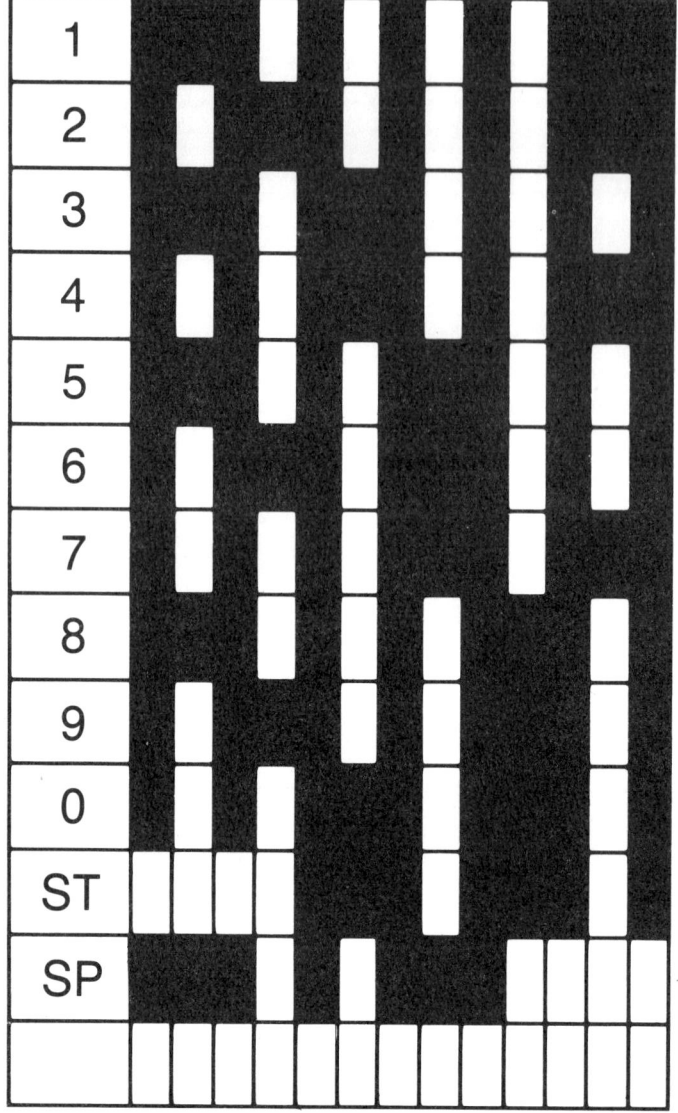

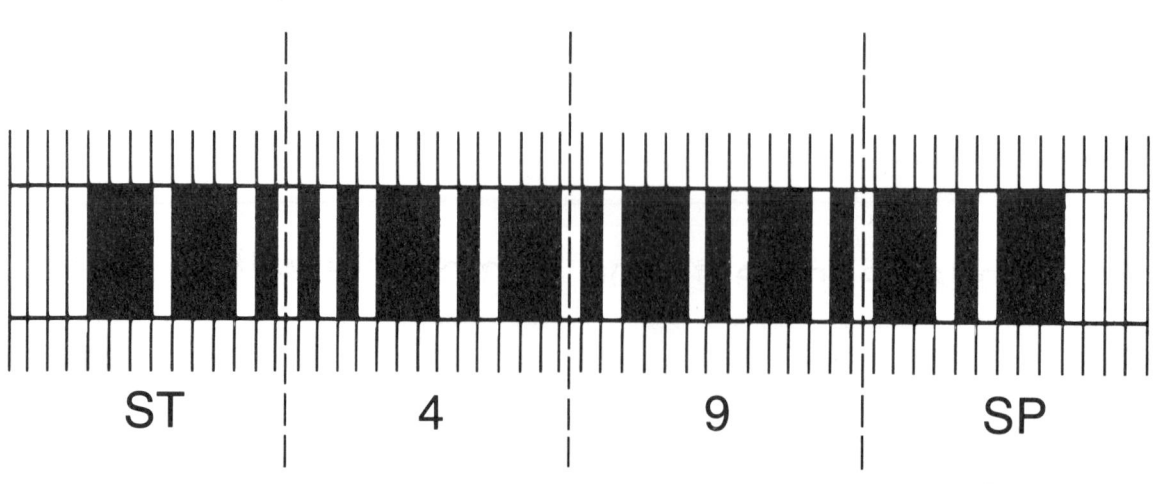

Bar Codes 3

To compress the space taken by the code, we use the spaces between the bars to form code as well as the bars themselves. This is called
interleaved 2 of 5

The format for characters 1–0 remains the same but start/stop characters are changed to shorter forms.

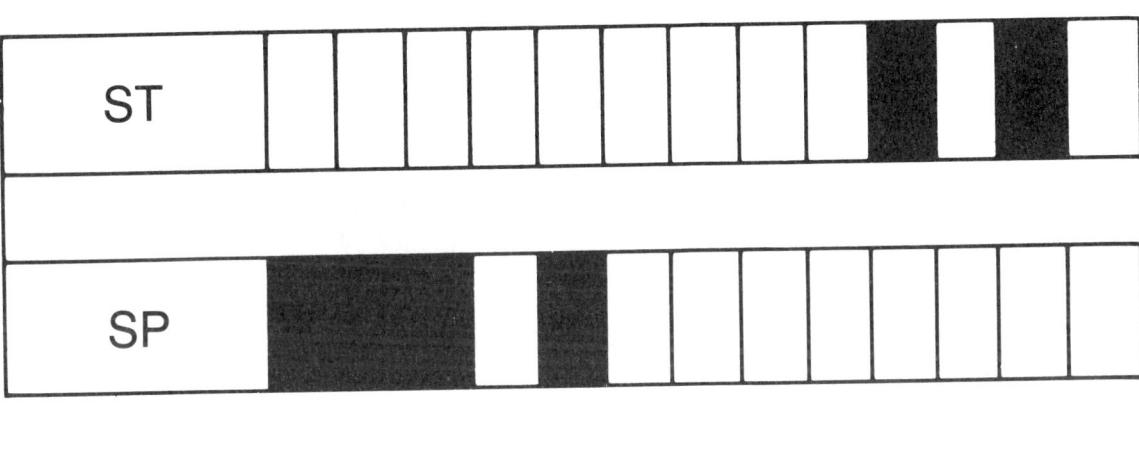

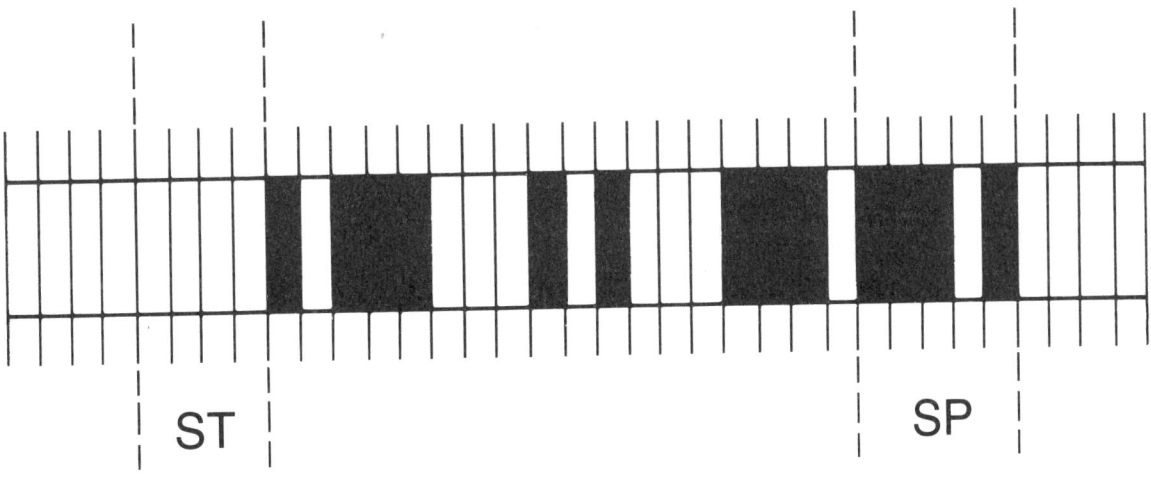

This code represents the number 29 with 2 made from the black bars and 9 made from the white bars.

An Example of the 2 in 5 Interleaved Bar Code

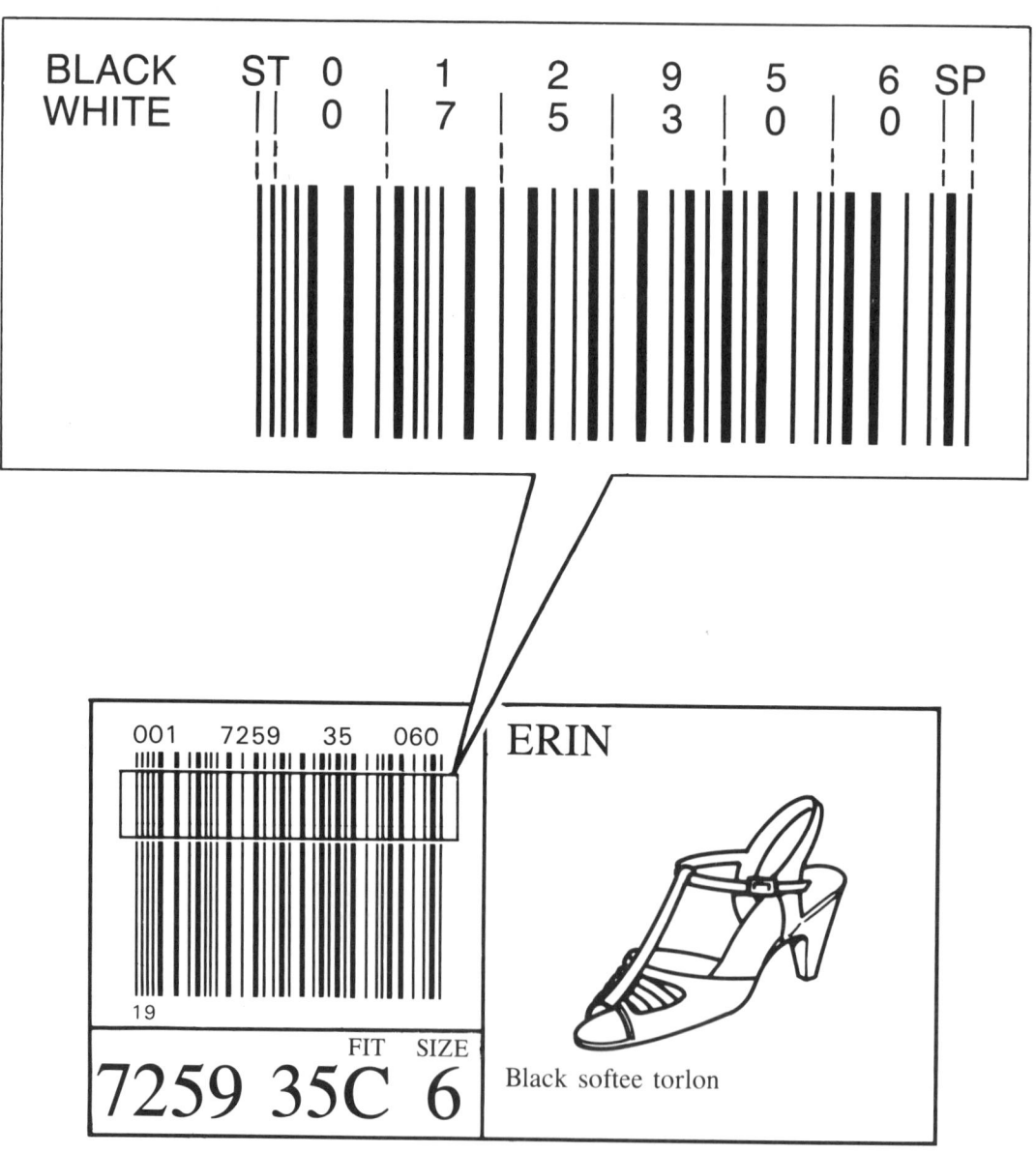

CHAPTER 3 | Processing and output

In order that students should get some 'user' feel for processing at a fairly early stage, we have started Chapter 3 by reference to a BASIC program, BIRTHDAY.BAS, which is one of those supplied on the disk associated with the text and which is printed at the end of this chapter. But this immediately introduces the concept of an interpreter program and different language levels.

This is perhaps no bad thing, because the BASIC interpreter sits nicely alongside COMMAND.COM on the overlay transparency, FS2.8e, to which we referred at the end of the last chapter. Being an interpreter, it must be executable at operating system level – i.e. its instructions must be written in binary code.

Reference back to Transparency FS2.4 may be useful here, for of the three categories of systems software, students have already acquired some appreciation of the operating system and have used one or two system utilities. Now they are introduced to an interpreter.

Transparency sequence 3.1 attempts to deal with language levels and the need for interpreters, ending with a distinction between *interpreters* and *compilers*. Within this sequence there is a set of overlays which allow the successive development of a pseudo set of three instructions in binary code, through Hex to Assembly language and then on to a simple BASIC statement, which achieves the same end. If you decide to use this set of overlays at this stage, we suggest that your treatment should be simplistic, dwelling not on the detail of instruction sets, but rather on the need for and use of successive language levels. You could refer back to the same foils again at a later stage, if and when you have developed students' grasp of binary and hexadecimal systems.

One of the features which becomes apparent to students as they use the BIRTHDAY.BAS program is that the commands and syntax are now controlled by the BASIC interpreter and not by COMMAND.COM. We believe this point is made fairly strongly in the student text, but we have stopped short of drawing attention to the fact that COMMAND.COM is still resident. Depending on your student groups, you may wish to make this point and (if appropriate to your hardware and software) to build on it, by introducing the use of other memory-resident software such as Borland's Sidekick, which on IBM PC XT/AT look-alike systems is available at any time, simply by pressing ALT + CTRL.

There may be other opportunities later to link back to this aspect of software remaining resident whilst control lies elsewhere, depending on the packages you are using. For example, Lotus

1–2–3 spreadsheet software allows temporary excursions back to the operating system; so does Paradox database software. A few word processing packages offer this facility too. But if you are using more limited hardware and software, such facilities will not be available and are probably best left unmentioned.

BIRTHDAY.BAS introduces the following key concepts:
- ☐ A *file*, with its constituent *fields* and *records*.
- ☐ The process of *input validation*.
- ☐ Some aspects of *records processing*.
- ☐ It is *menu-driven*.

Although these concepts are, in our view, handled adequately at an introductory level in the student text, you may wish to extend the work further with some students. For example, we do not explore the relative merits of menu-driven and command-driven software in the student text. You may wish to enlarge on this and explain that whilst progressing through menu layers can be frustrating to a user who knows the software well and who would rather get to the part he requires by one simple command, it is very helpful to those less familiar with the software. Such beginners are common in business environments because of staff turnover, promotions, etc. and software tends to be written to meet their needs.

The second point provides considerable opportunity for tutorial support, and as ever, the level to which you take it will depend on your students. Some things are appropriate for everybody – e.g. a revision of the analogy of the disk to a filing cabinet drawer, which was dealt with in Chapter 2, extending it now to look at the contents of a particular file, BIRTHDAY.DTA. We may visualize our folder in the filing cabinet drawer, as containing individual record cards, one for each of the friends whose birthday details we are keeping. Each record is kept in exactly the same format – the same category of data goes in the same place on each card. With this the analogy with the fields and records of a computer-generated file is complete. We have not included transparency masters relating to this analogy, because we feel you may well prefer to use actual physical objects as visual aids. Transparencies indicating fields and records within a file structure will be found in Sequence 4.3.

You may wish your students to see exactly how the data is held in the file BIRTHDAY.DTA and this is a good chance to use the system internal command, TYPE. If an individual has more than a screenful of records, you also have the chance to show one or more methods appropriate to your own systems for scroll locking (e.g. CTRL S) or for using a line-counting piece of software such as the system utility MORE.COM, often provided with MSDOS, to facilitate reading one screenful at a time.

If you do use the command TYPE BIRTHDAY.DTA, the display will show:

1. The use of inverted commas inserted automatically by the system as delimiters.
2. That the records are held as variable length records, each being separated from its neighbour by carrier return/line feed characters. These are of course provided by the user to indicate the end of a record, when inputting data.

We feel it is too early to get involved in a discussion as to why it is sometimes necessary to have fixed length records; suffice it at this stage, merely to note that the use of variable length records reduces the amount of disk and memory space taken up by the file.

The third point that you may wish to expand on is that of input validation. In BIRTHDAY.BAS the validation checks are very simple, merely ensuring that a selected option is called by a valid character; with a bright group of students you could develop an *algorithm* for checking the validity of every date at the time of input. Broadly, it might look something like this:

- ☐ Let input date be a string of the form *ddmmyy*.
- ☐ Check that the string length is exactly 6 characters.
- ☐ The value of *yy* cannot exceed 99.
- ☐ The value of *mm* cannot exceed 12.
- ☐ If the value of *mm* is 4 or 6 or 9 or 11 then the value of *dd* cannot exceed 30.
- ☐ If the value of *mm* is 2 and the integer part of (1900 + value of *yy*)/4 <> (1900 + value of *yy*)/4 then the value of *dd* cannot exceed 28. (An alternative statement of the condition is that (1900 + value of *yy*)/4 shall produce a non-zero remainder.)
- ☐ If the value of *mm* is 2 and the integer part of (1900 + value of *yy*)/4 = (1900 + value of *yy*)/4 then the value of *dd* cannot exceed 29. (Alternatively, the condition may be stated as: If the remainder resulting from (1900 + value of *yy*)/4 is zero, then . . .)
- ☐ In all other cases, the value of *dd* cannot exceed 31.

Especially if your students are going to try their hands at programming, it is important to take all possible opportunities to encourage them to develop algorithms before attempting coding. It is very common to find enthusiastic young people hammering in code, without first stopping to consider the system they are trying to model. The resulting program may well perform correctly, but the means by which the end has been achieved may be absolutely horrific in terms of computing practice. Good structure is vitally important and must be taught from the outset. But even if your students are not expected to sample programming, some assignments developing algorithms may well be worthwhile, because such work develops powers of analysis and logical thought.

There is another assignment they could attempt in the area of input validation; it is concerned with the use of check digits in such cases as bank account numbers, stock numbers, mail order catalogue numbers etc. If it is decided to cover this work, we feel it is important that students realize that there are many different systems of computing check digits, so that any work you undertake with them is illustrative rather than definitive. In Appendix 1, in Sequence FS3 you will find a group of three transparency masters which may be used as overlays in illustration of a simple check digit computation. This example is also given in Chapter 7 of the student text.

In this illustration we are considering a stock number. It could equally as well have been a catalogue number; either way, it is a known piece of data and the purpose of the check digit is to enable erroneous inputting of the number to be detected. As soon as the computer repeats the calculation by which the check digit was first calculated and finds that the recalculated check digit differs from the one which was input, the error is located. Check digits used in such applications will trap all common inputting errors.

Check digits are also used in much more exciting applications – for example as verification codes in the electronic transfer of high value sums of money. Another application is in the area of data transmission over a local or wide area network, where check digits are system-generated and relate to data length and content. In both these examples, the data is not a known character string, needing its accuracy checked as in the case of the stock or catalogue number; rather, it is an unpredictable quantity and in such cases, the object of the exercise is to verify that the received data is identical to the sent data. Transparency sequence 8.1 is also associated with data validation and is to be found at the end of Chapter 8.

The final feature noted as one on which you may wish to elaborate, concerns records processing. BIRTHDAY.BAS allows students to append records to a file in batches of up to 30, but to keep it simple, we do not sort the filed data; it remains in the order in which it was input. There is therefore no simple basis for merging records into appropriate position in file. But with suitable students, you might want to explore an algorithm for a natural merge of two files to produce a single sorted file. This is certainly going well beyond introductory level, but we simply wish to show a few of the developmental possiblities which abound in Information Technology and can grow from an introductory text like this one.

A more straightforward algorithm can be developed for the deletion of a record. It might look something like this:
- ☐ Identify the record to be deleted.
- ☐ Open the file containing the records and corresponding empty temporary file.
- ☐ While not end of data file, do the following:
    read a record;
    if it is *not* identical to the record which is to be deleted, write it to the temporary file,
    . . . until all records have been read.
- ☐ Delete contents of the data file.
- ☐ Copy the temporary file contents to the data file.
- ☐ Kill the temporary file.

Transparency sequence 3.2 gives a flowchart which corresponds with this algorithm.

The remainder of Chapter 3 is concerned with output from the computer, and we have put some emphasis on practical ability. Not all syllabuses which may be followed by students using our text will lay such emphasis on practical detail. However, these skills will certainly be required in working life, and such topics are required for courses preparing students for modules in the CGLI 726 Information Technology Series. We have included a few transparency masters in Sequence 3.3, which may be helpful when dealing with matrix and daisywheel printer principles.

In networked environments where there will probably be only one or two printers serving perhaps 15 work stations, we feel it is important that each student gets the chance to perform such simple tasks as changing daisywheels and ribbons, fitting sheet and/or tractor feeds, loading paper and so on.

In case it might be helpful, we have listed the program for BIRTHDAY.BAS on the following pages. It is not fully documented, but is, we believe, sufficiently simple in structure to follow without full documentation. This program uses syntax which is acceptable to GWBASIC and IBM BASICA amongst others.

The BIRTHDAY.BAS program

```
100 REM Program name: BIRTHDAY
110 REM Written by L F Cowan, Information Processing Services Ltd., Oxford.
120 REM Version 1.0: 1985 October 01
130 REM
140 REM
150 REM This program is designed to allow the user to compile a file of friends'
160 REM names and their birthdays, and subsequently to interrogate the file.
170 REM It is intended as an introduction to simple database concepts, and the
180 REM file constructed can also be used in later training exercises concerned
190 REM with sorting techniques.
200 REM
210 REM
220 REM
230 DIM SURNAME$(30),FIRST$(30),BIRTH$(30),LETTER$(30),CODE(30)
240 Z=0
250 WHILE Z<>5
260 CLS:K=0
270 PRINT :PRINT TAB(25);"B I R T H D A Y   L I S T"
280 PRINT :PRINT :PRINT TAB(12);"This software enables you to build up and inter
rogate"
290 PRINT TAB(12);"a database of your friends' birthdays."
300 PRINT :PRINT :PRINT TAB(12);"AVAILABLE OPTIONS:"
310 PRINT :PRINT TAB(12);"1.   Enter new names and birthdays"
320 PRINT :PRINT TAB(12);"2.   Delete entries"
330 PRINT :PRINT TAB(12);"3.   Interrogate data file"
335 PRINT :PRINT TAB(12);"4.   List all records on file"
340 PRINT :PRINT TAB(12);"5.   Exit from the program"
350 LOCATE 23,12
360 PRINT "PLEASE ENTER OPTION NUMBER (1, 2, 3, 4 or 5): "
370 Z$=INKEY$: IF Z$="" THEN 370
380 IF Z$="1" OR Z$="2" OR Z$="3" OR Z$="4" OR Z$="5" THEN 410 ELSE 390
390 PRINT CHR$(7);
400 GOTO 350
410 Z=VAL(Z$)
420 ON Z GOSUB 1000,2000,3000,4000
430 WEND
440 CLS
450 LOCATE 10,12
460 PRINT "YOU HAVE OPTED TO LEAVE THE PROGRAM.   ARE YOU SURE?  ";
470 Z$=INKEY$:IF Z$="" THEN 470
480 IF ASC(Z$)=89 OR ASC(Z$)=121 THEN SYSTEM
490 IF ASC(Z$)=78 OR ASC(Z$)=110 THEN 240
500 PRINT CHR$(7);
510 GOTO 440
520 REM
1000 REM **** ENTRIES OF NEW NAMES AND BIRTHDAYS ****
1010 REM
1020 REM
1030 K=K+1
1040 CLS
1050 PRINT :PRINT :PRINT TAB(26);"BIRTHDAY LIST - NEW ENTRIES"
1060 PRINT :PRINT :PRINT TAB(26);"SURNAME?   ";
1070 INPUT "",SURNAME$(K)
1080 WORDS$=SURNAME$(K):GOSUB 5000
1090 SURNAME$(K)=REMAKE$
1100 PRINT :PRINT TAB(26);"FIRST NAME?   ";
1110 INPUT "",FIRST$(K)
1120 WORDS$=FIRST$(K):GOSUB 5000
1130 FIRST$(K)=REMAKE$
1140 PRINT :PRINT TAB(26);"BIRTH DATE? (dd/mm/yy)   "
1150 PRINT TAB(26);"(It is important to use this format)"
1160 LOCATE 10,50
1170 INPUT "",BIRTH$(K)
1180 LOCATE 20,26
1190 PRINT "CHECK!  Are these entries correct?   (Y/N)   ";
1200 Z$=INKEY$:IF Z$="" THEN 1200
1210 IF ASC(Z$)=89 OR ASC(Z$)=121 THEN 1250
1220 IF ASC(Z$)=78 OR ASC(Z$)=110 THEN 1040
```

```
1230 PRINT CHR$(7)
1240 GOTO 1180
1250 LOCATE 23,26
1260 PRINT "More entries to make?   (Y/N)    ";
1270 Z$=INKEY$:IF Z$="" THEN 1270
1280 IF ASC(Z$)=89 OR ASC(Z$)=121 THEN IF K<>30 THEN 1000 ELSE 1300
1290 IF NOT(ASC(Z$)=78 OR ASC(Z$)=110) THEN PRINT CHR$(7):GOTO 1250
1300 OPEN "A:BIRTHDAY.DTA" FOR APPEND AS 1
1310 FOR J=1 TO K
1320 WRITE #1,SURNAME$(J),FIRST$(J),BIRTH$(J)
1330 NEXT J
1340 CLOSE #1
1350 IF K=30 AND (ASC(Z$)=89 OR ASC(Z$)=121) THEN K=0:GOTO 1000
1360 RETURN
1370 REM
2000 REM **** SUBROUTINE FOR DELETION OF ENTRIES ****
2010 REM
2020 CLS
2030 PRINT :PRINT :PRINT TAB(26);"BIRTHDAY LIST - DELETION OF ENTRIES"
2040 PRINT :PRINT :PRINT "WHAT IS THE SURNAME IN THE RECORD TO BE DELETED?   ";
2050 INPUT "",DELNAME$
2060 WORDS$=DELNAME$:GOSUB 5000
2070 DELNAME$=REMAKE$
2080 LOCATE 18,20
2090 PRINT"File search in progress.  Please wait..."
2100 OPEN "A:BIRTHDAY.DTA" FOR INPUT AS 1
2110 OPEN "A:TEMPFILE.$$$" FOR APPEND AS 2
2120 WHILE NOT(EOF(1))
2130 INPUT #1,SURNAME$,FIRST$,BIRTH$
2140 IF SURNAME$<>DELNAME$ THEN WRITE #2,SURNAME$,FIRST$,BIRTH$
2150 IF SURNAME$=DELNAME$ THEN GOSUB 2510
2160 WEND
2170 IF EOF(1) AND DELNAME$<>"*" THEN PRINT :PRINT "THERE IS NO RECORD OF THE RE
QUIRED PERSON ON FILE."
2180 IF EOF(1) AND DELNAME$="*" THEN PRINT :PRINT TAB(20);"Record being deleted.
    Please wait..."
2190 CLOSE #1
2200 CLOSE #2
2210 KILL "A:BIRTHDAY.DTA"
2220 OPEN "A:BIRTHDAY.DTA" FOR APPEND AS 1
2230 OPEN "A:TEMPFILE.$$$" FOR INPUT AS 2
2240 WHILE NOT(EOF(2))
2250 INPUT #2,SURNAME$,FIRST$,BIRTH$
2260 WRITE #1,SURNAME$,FIRST$,BIRTH$
2270 WEND
2280 CLOSE #1
2290 CLOSE #2
2300 KILL "A:TEMPFILE.$$$"
2310 RETURN
2320 REM
2500 REM
2510 REM **** PREVENTS TRANSFER OF UNWANTED RECORD TO RECONSTRUCTED FILE ****
2520 REM
2530 PRINT :PRINT :PRINT "PLEASE CONFIRM THAT YOU WISH TO REMOVE ";FIRST$;" ";SU
RNAME$
2540 PRINT "FROM THE FILE (Y/N)    ";
2550 Z$=INKEY$:IF Z$="" THEN 2550
2560 IF ASC(Z$)=89 OR ASC(Z$)=121 THEN DELNAME$="*":GOTO 2620
2570 IF ASC(Z$)=78 OR ASC(Z$)=110 THEN WRITE #2,SURNAME$,FIRST$,BIRTH$:GOTO 2620
2580 PRINT CHR$(7)
2590 CLS
2600 LOCATE 8,1
2610 GOTO 2510
2620 RETURN
3000 REM **** INTERROGATION OF DATA FILE ****
3010 REM
3020 REM
3030 CLS
3040 PRINT :PRINT TAB(30);"BIRTHDAY LIST - ENQUIRIES"
3050 PRINT :PRINT TAB(10);"You may ask for the birthdate of a named (I)ndividual
 or list"
3060 PRINT TAB(10);"all individuals whose birthdays occur in a named (M)onth."
3070 PRINT :PRINT :PRINT TAB(10);"PLEASE ENTER I OR M ... ";
3080 Z=0
3090 Z$=INKEY$:IF Z$="" THEN 3090
3100 IF ASC(Z$)=73 OR ASC(Z$)=105 THEN Z=1
3110 IF ASC(Z$)=77 OR ASC(Z$)=109 THEN Z=2
3120 IF NOT(Z=1 OR Z=2) THEN PRINT CHR$(7):GOTO 3090
3130 OPEN "A:BIRTHDAY.DTA" FOR INPUT AS 1
3140 ON Z GOSUB 3300,3600
3150 REM Subroutine 3300 searches the file for the record of a named individual.
3160 REM subroutine 3600 searches the file for all records in which the 4th and
3170 REM 5th characters in the birth date field correspond with the named month.
3180 CLOSE #1
3190 LOCATE 23,10
3200 PRINT"(M)ore enquiries or (R)eturn to the main menu?   ";
3210 Z$=INKEY$:IF Z$="" THEN 3210
3220 IF ASC(Z$)=77 OR ASC(Z$)=109 THEN 3030
3230 IF ASC(Z$)=82 OR ASC(Z$)=114 THEN 3260
3240 PRINT CHR$(7)
3250 GOTO 3210
3260 RETURN
3270 REM
```

```
3300 REM **** FILE SEARCH FOR NAMED INDIVIDUAL & CHECK ON VALIDITY ****
3310 REM
3320 PRINT :PRINT :PRINT "WHOSE BIRTH DATE DO YOU WANT?  Please enter SURNAME: ";
3330 INPUT"",WANTED$
3340 WORDS$=WANTED$:GOSUB 5000:REM Converts input to upper case.
3350 WANTED$=REMAKE$
3360 WANTED=0
3370 WHILE (NOT(EOF(1)) AND NOT(WANTED))
3380 INPUT #1,SURNAME$,FIRST$,BIRTH$
3390 IF SURNAME$=WANTED$ THEN PRINT :PRINT TAB(15);"Please confirm that you want the birth" ELSE 3460
3400 IF SURNAME$=WANTED$ THEN PRINT TAB(15);"date of ";FIRST$;" ";SURNAME$;" (Y/N) "
3410 Z$=INKEY$:IF Z$="" THEN 3410
3420 IF ASC(Z$)=89 OR ASC(Z$)=121 THEN WANTED=-1:GOTO 3460
3430 IF ASC(Z$)=78 OR ASC(Z$)=110 THEN 3460
3440 PRINT CHR$(7)
3450 GOTO 3410
3460 WEND
3470 IF EOF(1) AND WANTED=0 THEN PRINT :PRINT "THE BIRTH DATE REQUESTED IS NOT ON FILE."
3480 IF WANTED=-1 THEN PRINT:PRINT"THE BIRTH DATE OF ";FIRST$;" ";SURNAME$;" IS ";BIRTH$
3490 RETURN
3500 REM
3600 REM **** FILE SEARCH FOR ALL RECORDS WITH DATE FIELD CONTAINING NAMED MONTH ****
3610 REM
3620 PRINT :PRINT :PRINT "FOR WHICH MONTH DO YOU WANT A LISTING OF BIRTHDAYS? "
3630 PRINT "(Please enter the first three letters of the month, eg Jan, Feb, etc)"
3640 LOCATE 10,53
3650 INPUT "",MONTH$
3660 WORDS$=MONTH$:GOSUB 5000:REM Converts input to upper case.
3670 MONTH$=REMAKE$
3680 IF MONTH$="JAN" THEN MONTH=1
3690 IF MONTH$="FEB" THEN MONTH=2
3700 IF MONTH$="MAR" THEN MONTH=3
3710 IF MONTH$="APR" THEN MONTH=4
3720 IF MONTH$="MAY" THEN MONTH=5
3730 IF MONTH$="JUN" THEN MONTH=6
3740 IF MONTH$="JUL" THEN MONTH=7
3750 IF MONTH$="AUG" THEN MONTH=8
3760 IF MONTH$="SEP" THEN MONTH=9
3770 IF MONTH$="OCT" THEN MONTH=10
3780 IF MONTH$="NOV" THEN MONTH=11
3790 IF MONTH$="DEC" THEN MONTH=12
3800 P=0
3810 WHILE NOT(EOF(1))
3820 INPUT #1,SURNAME$,FIRST$,BIRTH$
3830 IF VAL(MID$(BIRTH$,4,2))=MONTH THEN P=P+1:SURNAME$(P)=SURNAME$:FIRST$(P)=FIRST$:BIRTH$(P)=BIRTH$
3840 WEND
3850 PRINT STRING$(3,10);"THE FOLLOWING BIRTHDAYS OCCUR IN THE SPECIFIED MONTH:"
3860 PRINT
3870 FOR Q=1 TO P
3880 PRINT TAB(17);FIRST$(Q);" ";SURNAME$(Q);"'S BIRTH DATE IS ";BIRTH$(Q)
3890 NEXT Q
3900 RETURN
3910 REM
4000 REM **** SUBROUTINE TO LIST ALL RECORDS ON FILE ****
4010 REM
4020 REM
4030 CLS
4040 LOCATE 5,10
4050 PRINT "YOU HAVE OPTED TO LIST ALL RECORDS ON FILE."
4060 PRINT :PRINT TAB(10);"Do you wish the output to go to (P)rinter or to (S)creen?"
4070 PRINT TAB(10);"Please type P or S....  ";
4080 Y$=INKEY$:IF Y$="" THEN 4080
4090 IF NOT(ASC(Y$)=80 OR ASC(Y$)=112 OR ASC(Y$)=83 OR ASC(Y$)=115) THEN PRINT CHR$(7):GOTO 4080
4100 IF ASC(Y$)=83 OR ASC(Y$)=115 THEN 4250:'(Routine for printing to screen)
4110 LOCATE 18,10
4120 PRINT "Please ensure that your printer is connected to the computer,"
4130 PRINT TAB(10);"switched on and loaded with paper."
4140 PRINT :PRINT TAB(10);"Press any key when ready to commence printing..."
4150 Y$=INKEY$:IF Y$="" THEN 4150
4160 CLS
4170 LOCATE 10,10
4180 PRINT "PRINTING IN PROGRESS ... PLEASE WAIT."
4185 LPRINT "LISTING OF ALL RECORDS HELD IN FILE BIRTHDAY.DTA":LPRINT
4190 OPEN "A:BIRTHDAY.DTA" FOR INPUT AS 1
4200 WHILE NOT(EOF(1))
4210 INPUT #1,SURNAME$,FIRST$,BIRTH$
4220 LPRINT SURNAME$;", ";FIRST$;TAB(35);BIRTH$
4230 WEND
4240 CLOSE #1:GOTO 4390
4250 CLS:N=0
4260 PRINT :PRINT TAB(20);"LISTING OF ALL RECORDS ON FILE"
4270 PRINT
4280 OPEN "A:BIRTHDAY.DTA" FOR INPUT AS 1
```

```
4290 WHILE NOT(EOF(1))
4300 INPUT #1,SURNAME$,FIRST$,BIRTH$
4310 PRINT TAB(10);SURNAME$;", ";FIRST$;TAB(45);BIRTH$
4320 N=N+1
4330 IF N=18 THEN GOSUB 4500
4340 WEND
4350 CLOSE #1
4360 LOCATE 23,10
4370 PRINT "The listing is complete.  To return to the main menu, press any key.
."
4380 Y$=INKEY$:IF Y$="" THEN 4380
4390 RETURN
4500 REM **** FULL SCREEN INTERRUPT ROUTINE ****
4510 REM
4520 REM
4530 LOCATE 23,10
4540 PRINT "The list continues.  To see more, press any key... "
4550 Y$=INKEY$:IF Y$="" THEN 4550
4560 CLS:N=0
4570 PRINT :PRINT TAB(20);"LISTING OF ALL RECORDS continued"
4580 PRINT
4590 RETURN
5000 REM **** SUBROUTINE TO CONVERT ALL ALPHA INPUTS TO UPPER CASE ****
5010 REM
5020 REM The string to be converted by this subroutine must have been assigned
5030 REM to the variable WORDS$ before entering the subroutine.  The first
5040 REM statement after returning from the subroutine must be a re-assignment
5050 REM from REMAKE$ to the original variable.
5060 REM
5070 REM
5080 REMAKE$=""
5090 FOR P=1 TO LEN(WORDS$)
5100 LETTER$(P)=MID$(WORDS$,P,1)
5110 CODE(P)=ASC(LETTER$(P))
5120 IF CODE(P)>96 AND CODE(P)<123 THEN CODE(P)=CODE(P)-32
5130 LETTER$(P)=CHR$(CODE(P))
5140 REMAKE$=REMAKE$+LETTER$(P)
5150 NEXT P
5160 RETURN
```

Chapter 3 – Transparency sequence 1
Basic principles for instructing a computer to undertake a simple operation

The following transparencies reinforce concepts illustrated in Sequence FS2.3 concerning the function of the control unit and the Arithmetic and Logic Unit (ALU) especially, and lead to an appreciation of language levels.

Notes

Transparency reference	3.1.1	A somewhat frivolous cartoon with a serious message – a machine can only understand machine code, and if we wish to instruct it to do something, we must do so in terms which it can handle. Ultimately this means electric voltage levels representing the 1s and 0s of binary code, but we are not concerned with the electrical aspects and stop at binary code.
3.1.1 and 3.1.2 appear on one page in this manual and will need photocopying individually before being made into transparencies.	3.1.2	The instructions we wish the computer to obey are set out on this transparency. Since we are starting at absolute basics, we are specifying designated memory locations. There are two major over-simplifications which you should recognize, but which will not affect the principles we are trying to get across. The first is that data would not be held in memory locations with such low addresses; the second is that a number could not be represented in a single byte; depending on the precision required, it could take up to four bytes. Furthermore, it would be held in standard form, there would be a sign digit and so on.

But our intention is not to obscure the principles by revealing detail which is of no real consequence to most users – certainly not the first time around.

3.1.3a–c   This series of three transparencies draws an analogy between the computer undertaking the instructions shown in 3.1.2 and a railway marshalling yard.

Start with 3.1.3a and immediately overlay 3.1.3b to show more of the signal box activity. The signal man has a list of jobs to be done (our instructions to the computer) and some standing rules always to be followed (such as certain kinds of tasks always having priority over other kinds of tasks). He has a clock, so that activities that need to be synchronized, can be and has a means of communication both within the railway system and to the outside world.

The four separate illustrations on 3.1.3c represent four trains, each with a header code, and they need to be cut out as individual pieces of (preferably coloured) transparency. The train with header 19 needs to be placed in siding 19; similarly trains 15 and 18 are placed in their sidings. Train V is not wanted yet.

Under the control of the signal man, you can now show the instructions of 3.1.2 in operation.

This done, you could move to the first part of 3.1.4, but keep the 3.1.3 assembly to hand, because we shall want it again in a minute.

3.1.4 This transparency should be made in four separate parts, each hinged at its left-hand or right-hand edge. The first part shows a possible binary code description of the operation (function and register associated with the function) followed by the address of the number on which the function is to operate.

The second part of the transparency shows the same codes and addresses written in Hex. (Hex is a convenient notation for computer engineers because the binary equivalent of any Hex character can be contained in exactly half a byte.) If we had to write in machine code, we would choose Hex notation rather than binary to convey the instructions.

Usually we are not concerned that a particular piece of data should be stored at a specific address; we would be happy if the computer looked after the detail.

Refer back to the 3.1.3 assembly and have the train headed V coming into the marshalling yard. What we are saying to the signalman is 'We know this train as V. You may put it in whatever siding you want, but you must remember where you place it so that every time we tell you to do something with V, you know where to find it.'

Combined with this advance of being able to refer to a storage location by the variable name of the data contained in it, is another step away from machine code: mnemonics replace operation codes, so that we might, for example, use LDA to mean LOAD the ACCUMULATOR, ADD to mean just that, and so on. Return to 3.1.4 and introduce the third part of this transparency, where the instructions to add one variable to another to produce a third are illustrated in an assembly language. The machine, of course, needs to be told that the group of characters LDA actually means A5 (Hex) or 10100101. Instructions containing such information are contained in a program called an *assembler*, which converts assembly language to machine code. It follows that the assembler is written in machine code.

Finally, introduce the fourth part of 3.1.4, where the same instruction is presented in BASIC.

3.1.5 This reinforces the function of an assembler, by comparing it with that of an interpreter and a compiler. The terms *source code* and *object code* are also introduced.

Chapter 3 – Transparency sequence 2
Flowchart to illustrate the algorithm for deleting a specified record from file

Notes

Transparency reference

3.2a You may like to overlay this with a transparency which temporarily covers the gap between the second and third boxes whilst you take students through operations described by the flowchart. Then remove this temporary overlay and replace it with the overlay 3.2.b in order to reinforce the description by reference to actual data.

3.2b   To save writing on this transparency, overlay it with a blank one. Then as an example, enter in the data file table some of the surnames used by students in their BIRTHDAY.DTA files. Select any one of them as the record which is to be deleted and enter it in that box.

Now you can follow the flowchart with each data item, gradually building up the contents of TEMPFILE as you progress through the records in the data file.

Chapter 3 – Transparency sequence 3
Matrix and daisywheel printer principles

As laser printers get cheaper and as 24-pin dot matrix printers produce even better letter quality output, daisywheel printers are becoming less widely used. Look around any major computer exhibition and see where the emphasis lies.

But of course, many users still have daisywheel printers giving high quality reliable, if noisy, output, and examination syllabuses will undoubtedly still cover daisywheels for years to come.

Notes

Transparency reference

3.3.1   The upper half shows a collection of daisywheels of different types; note the spigot hole for accurate location of the printwheel on the drive spindle.

The lower diagram illustrates the turning of the printwheel with the solenoid firing as the required character comes into line with it.

3.3.2   Matrix printer operation is easiest illustrated by reference to a 9-pin head, and certainly many of the matrix printers which students will come across will have this standard.

The upper diagram illustrates how individual characters are formed from successive strikes of different combinations of the pins as the head moves in very small increments across the platen.

One of the key virtues of matrix printers *vis-à-vis* daisywheels is their flexibility, and this is well illustrated in the lower picture, which was produced on a 9-pin matrix printer near the bottom of the price range.

3.3.3   The upper illustration shows some typical dot matrix characters, each set in a standard 9 × 6 matrix. Note that the right-hand column and bottom row in each character block is kept empty (except for the descender of lower case y) to give space between successive characters and lines.

The lower diagram shows the way horizontal increment is reduced to achieve 12-pitch or 17.5-pitch. Some systems using 9-pin heads also improve vertical dot density by very small incremental movements of the platen, but this makes the print speed very low. With a 24-pin head, the pins are much smaller in diameter and mounted in two 12-pin columns, in such a way that the second column is displaced vertically by half a dot pitch, relative to the first column. Thus, the density of dots vertically is much better with 24-pin heads than with 9-pin heads.

Instructing the Computer

To add two numbers and save the result, the machine would need instructions like:

- Load contents of location 15 into the accumulator
- Add contents of location 18 to contents of accumulator
- Store result from accumulator in location 19

An Analogy with the Central Processing Unit

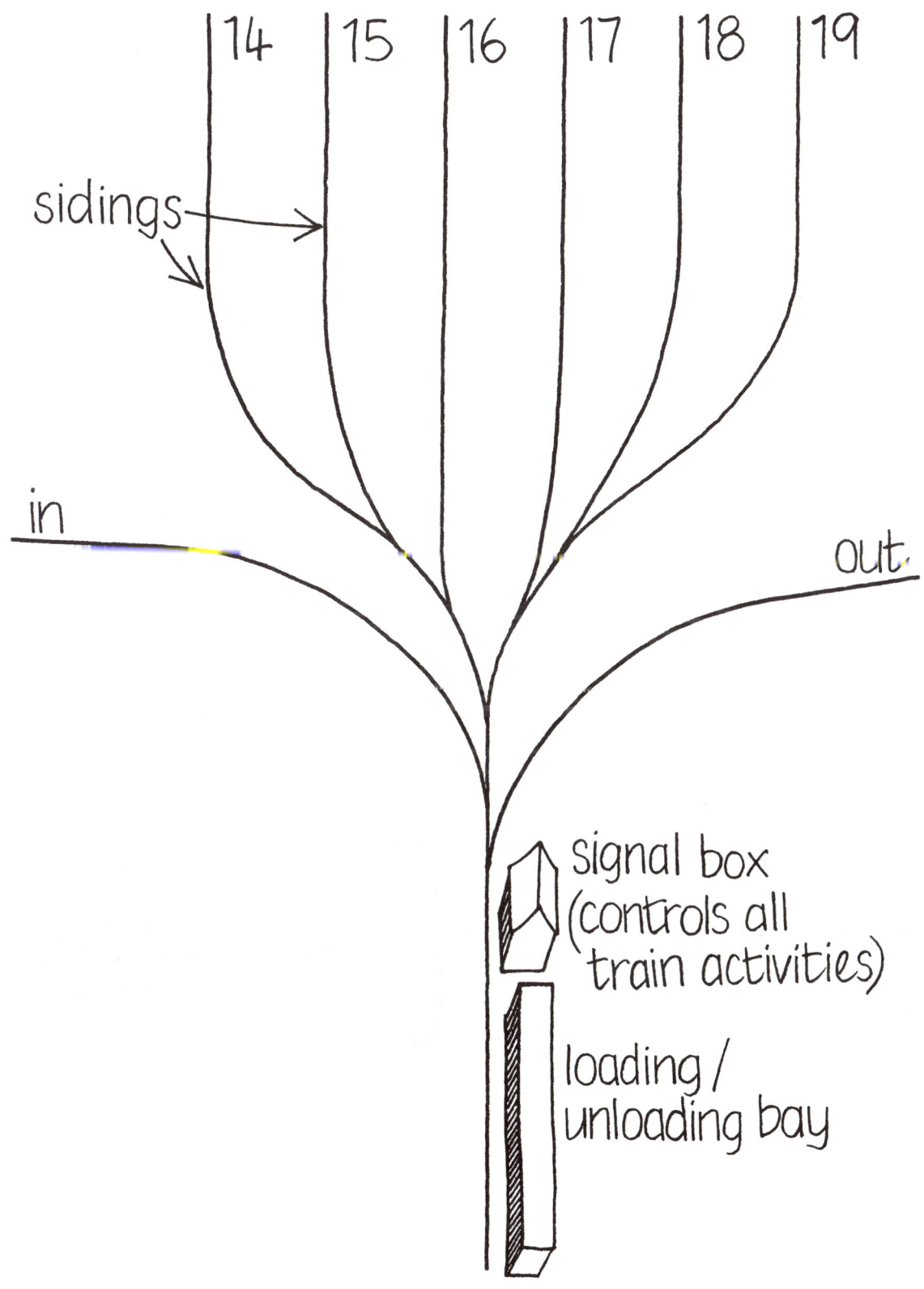

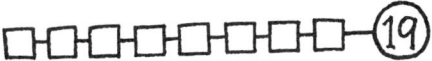

Different Language Levels

A typical binary code for these instructions might be

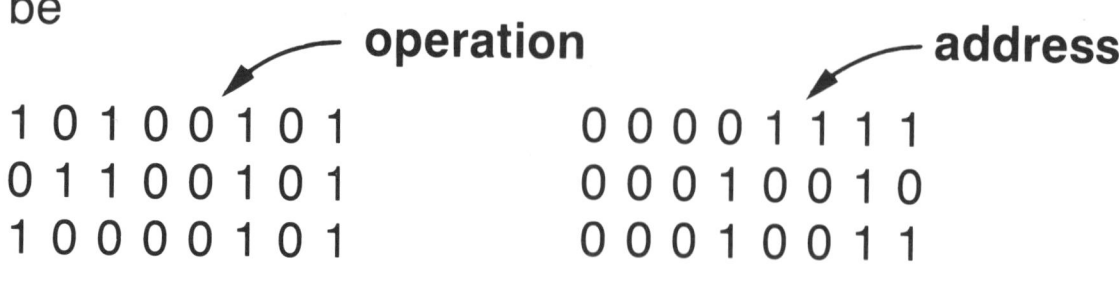

```
        operation              address
1 0 1 0 0 1 0 1        0 0 0 0 1 1 1 1
0 1 1 0 0 1 0 1        0 0 0 1 0 0 1 0
1 0 0 0 0 1 0 1        0 0 0 1 0 0 1 1
```

The same instruction in hexadecimal (HEX) would be

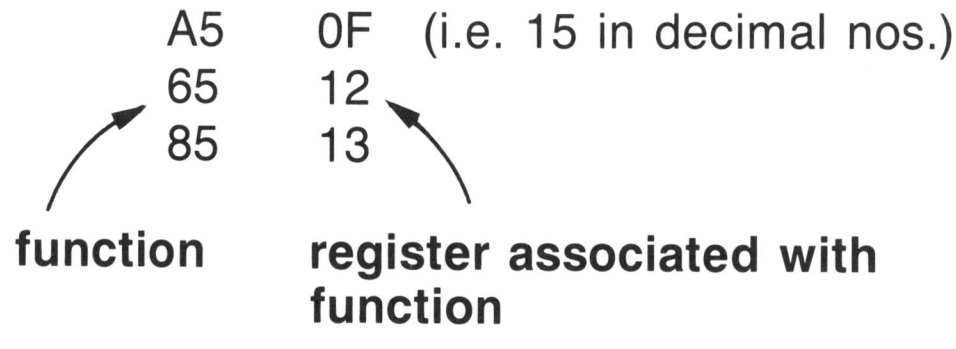

```
        A5    0F    (i.e. 15 in decimal nos.)
        65    12
        85    13
     function    register associated with
                 function
```

The same instruction in a typical Assembly Language might be

```
    { LDA   P }
    { ADD   V }   meaningful symbols
    { STA   T }   for memory locations
mnemonics replace        (e.g. Price before VAT)
operation codes          (     VAT            )
                         (     Total          )
```

The same instruction in a 'high level' language such as BASIC would be T = P + V

Assembly language is translated to binary machine code by a program called an *assembler*.

The same kind of process for a high-level language like BASIC is performed either by an *interpreter* or a *compiler*.

Interpreter translates the key-words in a high level language program line by line as the program runs. The program has to be interpreted each time it is run.

Compiler converts a complete program into a machine code version which can be stored and run whenever required.

(source code → object code)

Deleting a Record

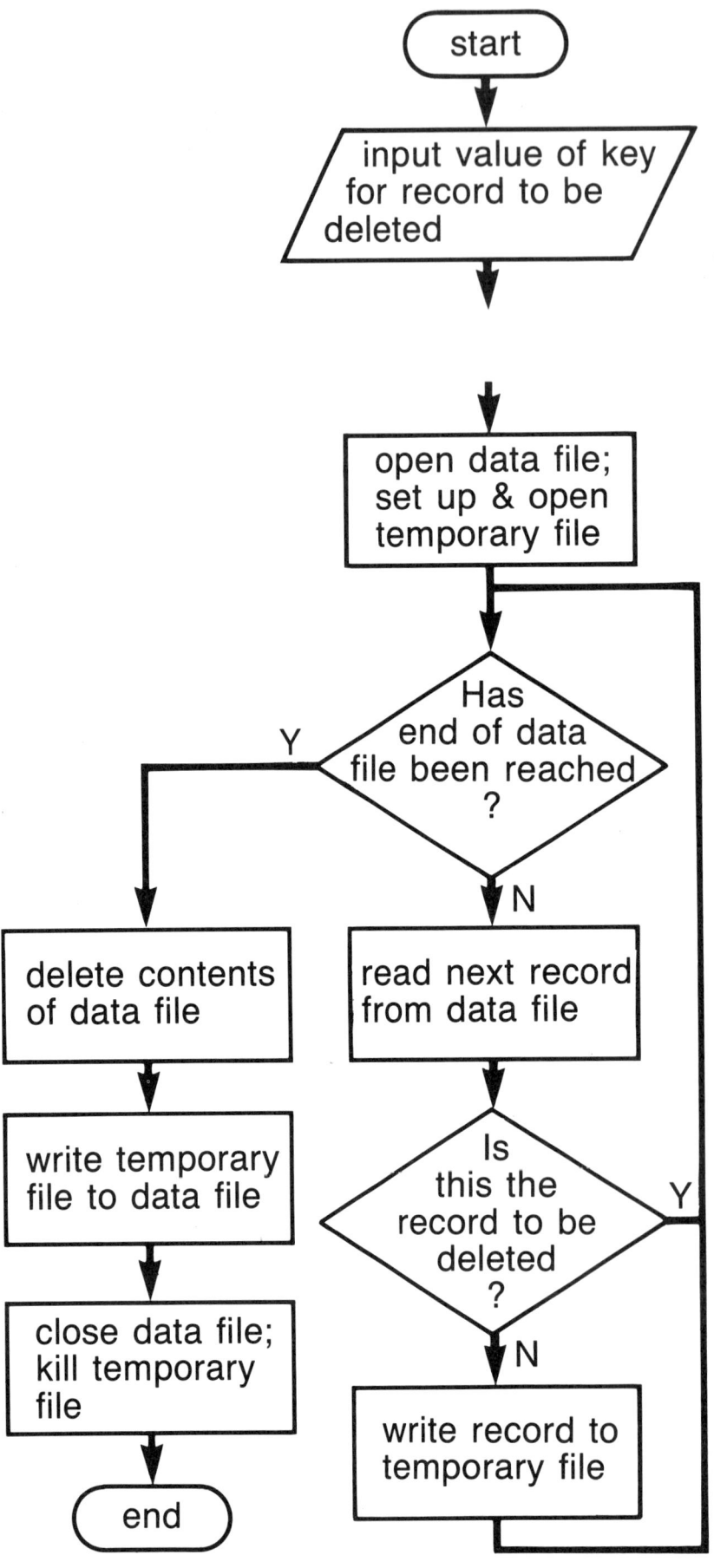

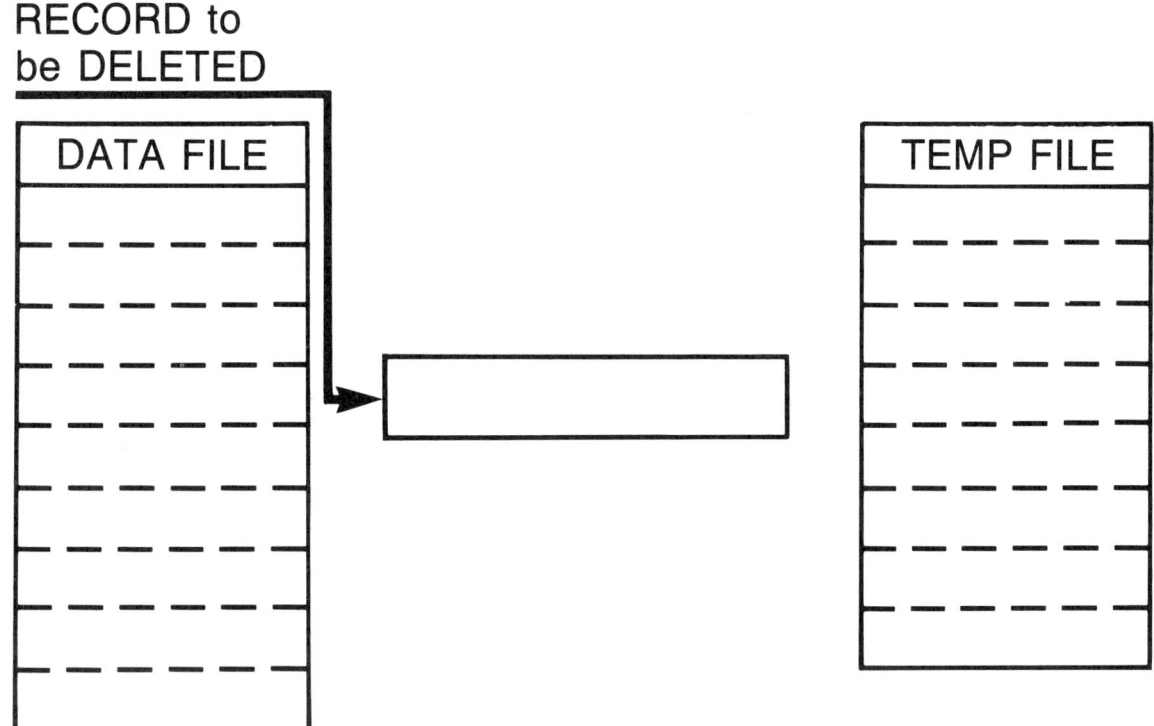

Daisywheels

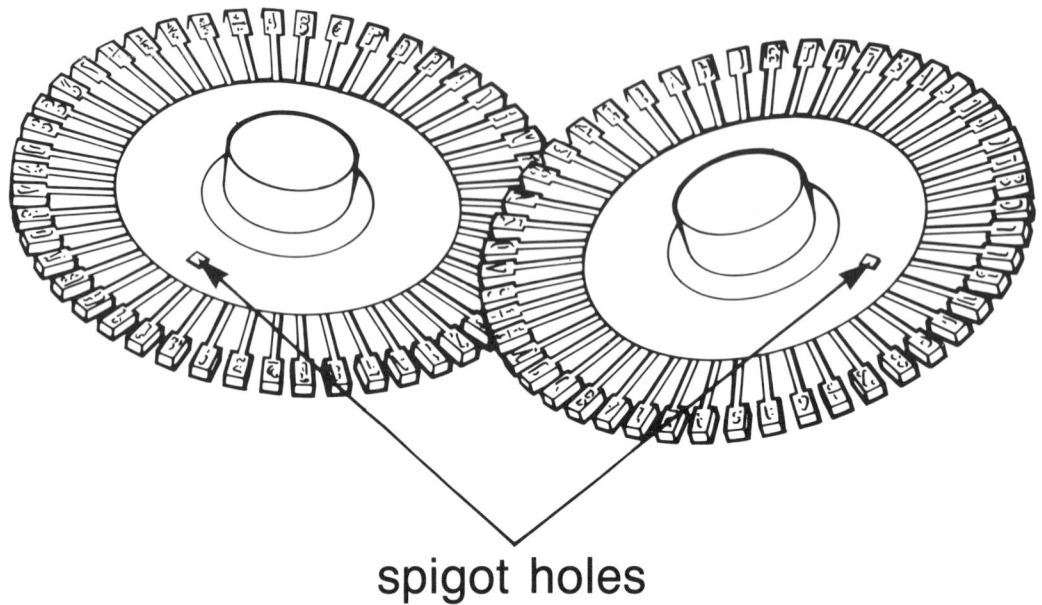

spigot holes

The movement of the daisywheel when printing

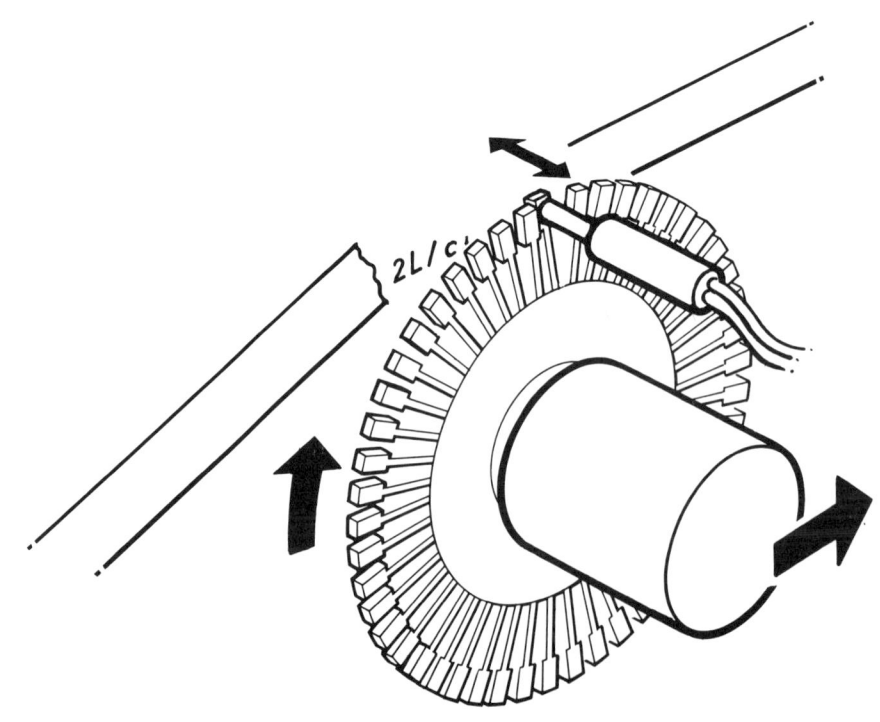

Matrix Printers

The movement of the matrix printer head when printing

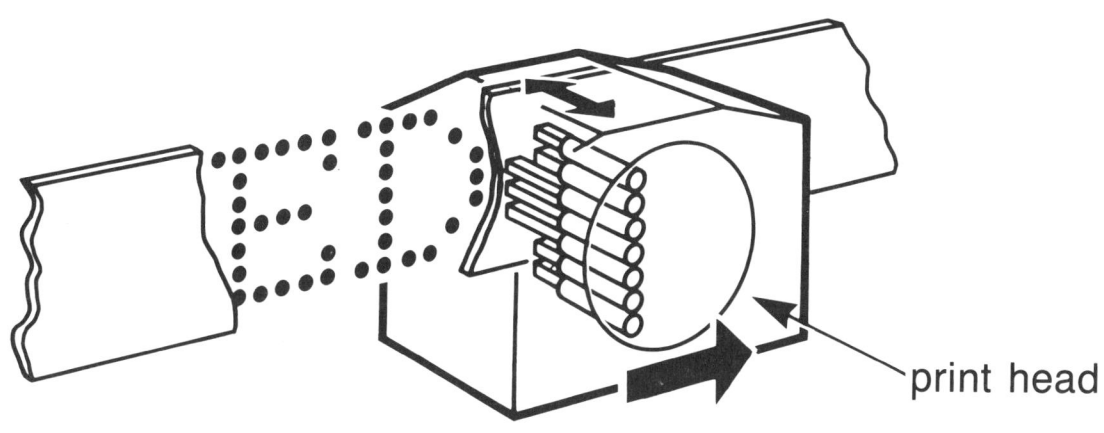

An image produced by a 9-pin matrix printer

Dot Matrix Characters

Dot matrix characters in a standard 9 × 6 matrix

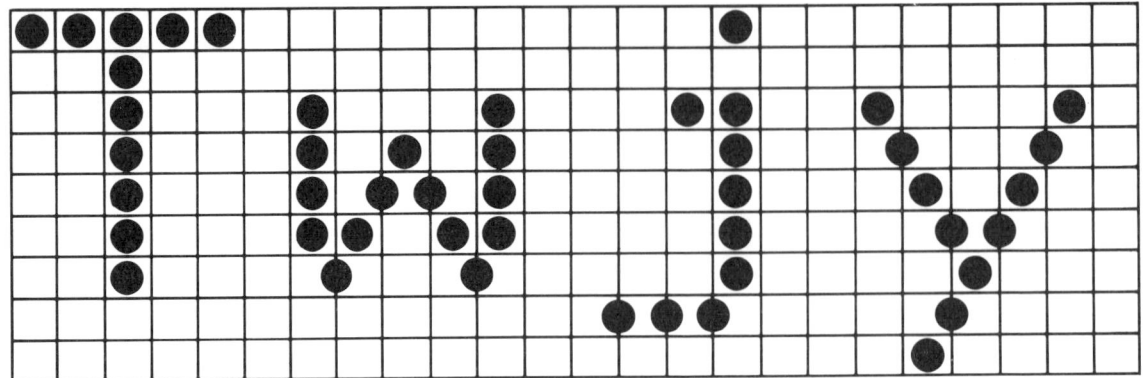

How dot density changes print style

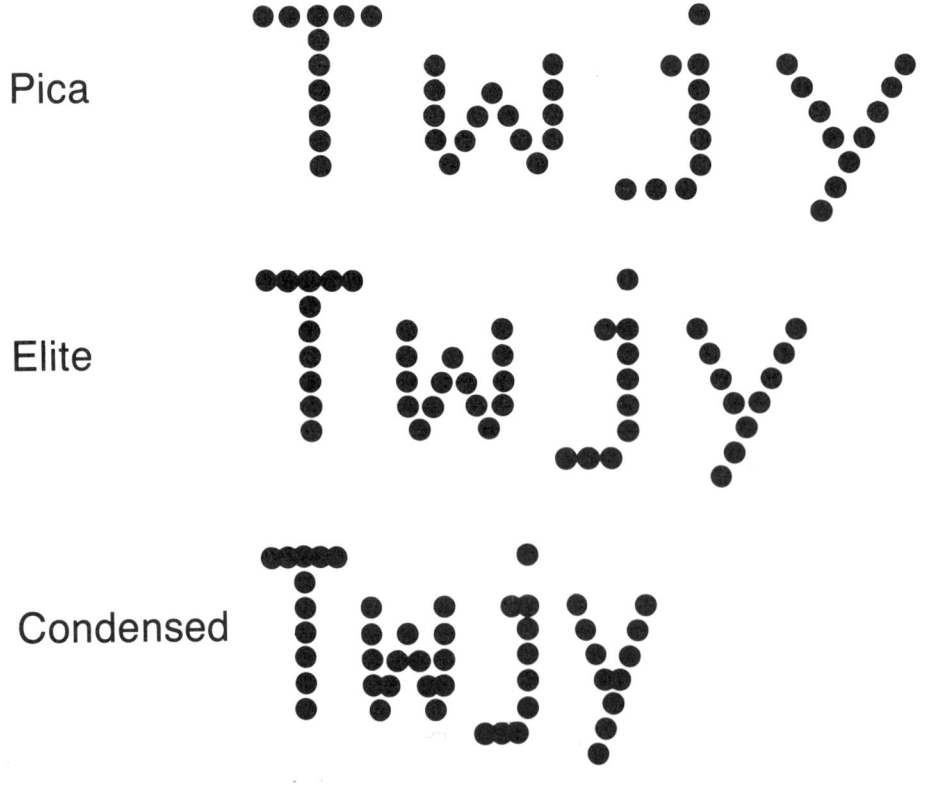

Pica

Elite

Condensed

CHAPTER 4 — First steps in database design and use

Early in this chapter of the student text, we seek to answer three basic questions:

1 What is a database?
2 How does it differ from a program-centred information system?
3 Of what advantage is a data-centred approach?

Transparency sequence 4.1 starts with these same questions and then broadens the approach to them somewhat.

The student text goes on to explore the nature of data, giving some emphasis to the way it relates to time. (Sequence 4.2 contains a number of transparencies extending concepts of data qualification; these details, not being in the mainstream of database work, do not figure in the Pupil's Book. However, if time permits, it is an avenue you can explore with appropriate students.)

After pointing out that data is, in general, time-sensitive, the student text makes passing reference to the need for job scheduling. This is one of the four essential functions of database administration, and in a text other than at introductory level, we would need to treat the whole topic of database administration much more rigorously. But our prime objective is to help students produce a small database and explore the facilities it offers, rather than to take the more formal approach, which is necessary if one is to set up a multi-user, multi-entity database with all necessary procedures and safeguards.

In the student text we distinguish clearly between data and information, and this is illustrated by reference to two totally different views of data which make up a telephone directory. A parallel illustration is provided in Sequence 4.3 in case you wish to handle this piece of work as a group exercise. The sequence illustrates fields and records, and introduces the term *key field*.

The remainder of the work in the database chapter is essentially practical, and we cannot usefully provide support material for it, because there are such wide variations in the many software packages which may be used.

In running this practical work, we would anticipate that you will encounter two main difficulties: the first will arise simply from students' unfamiliarity with the software and their lack of observation of screen prompts. We never cease to be amazed by the relatively large number of students – school-leavers and mature adults alike – who do not see half the information which is displayed on screen. It is vital that they learn to see it, and you may wish to take specific steps to encourage this, if you do not already do so.

The second point which will require your attention is to define for your students the cut-off point, in the work on the Club database. This will depend on the facility offered by your database software; for example, can it handle arithmetic processing?

Within the span of work which can be covered by the software available to you, there will be approaches quite unlike those available with Delta software, which we have used to exemplify various aspects of database use. Here you will need to work with your students to show how the particular aspects are handled using your software. Hopefully, the framework outlined in Chapter 4 of the student text will be sufficient to enable your students to achieve similar ends, though by different means.

We offer on the following pages a *pro forma* which may be helpful to you in this respect.

First steps in database construction and use

The database software you are using is: _____

1 Data definition

Once the database software is loaded, press _____ to obtain the screen allowing you to define your database. In response to screen prompts provide a file name for this file, which will hold the definitions you are about to create. File names may be up to eight characters in length and may not contain spaces. Field names may be up to _____ characters in length; spaces are/are not allowable in field names.

> Field types:
> For alphabetic or alphanumeric fields the field type code is _____; field length is the number of characters you expect to use for the longest data entry which is ever likely to be made in that field.
> For numeric fields, the field type code is _____ (the field length must/must not be specified as well).
> For date fields, the field type code is _____

When all fields have been defined, the definitions must be saved. The keystrokes for doing this are _____

2 Preparing a form (or 'mask') for data input

Press _____ to obtain the screen allowing you to build your own data input form. You may use the cursor (arrow) keys to move to any point on the screen and you may type in from the keyboard any textual prompts which you wish to use in your form.

To place a field on the form, use this procedure:

_____
_____
_____

3 Data entry through the prepared form
Use this key sequence to call your prepared form and use it for date entry: _____
_____

Each record/batch of records must be saved to disk and the procedure for doing this is: _____
_____
_____

4 Setting up selection criteria
Use these keystrokes to call a screen allowing you to enter your selection criteria: _____

These are examples of how to express selection criteria:

    a Indicating the field(s) to which selection criteria are to be applied: _____
_____

    b Selection on the basis of:
    equality: numbers _____
    dates _____
    text – exact _____
    text – ignoring upper/lower case _____
_____
_____

    inequality: numbers _____
    dates _____
    text – exact _____
    text – ignoring upper/lower case _____
_____

    greater than: numbers _____
    dates _____

    greater than or equal: numbers _____
    dates _____

    less than: numbers _____
    dates _____

less than or equal: numbers _____
dates _____

range between: numbers _____
dates _____

5 Choosing the fields to be displayed for the selected group of records: _____
_____
_____
_____

6 Extracting from the database those records which meet the selection criteria: _____
_____
_____
_____

7 Sorting the extracted records on one or more fields: _____
_____
_____
_____

8 With some database software you *must* save the extracted records in a disk file; in other cases you need not, but may opt to do so if you wish. The procedure for saving the extracted records in a file is: _____
_____
_____
_____

9 Designing the output report
Page width is adjusted by this key sequence: _____
_____
_____

The size of fields as printed may be adjusted by: _____
_____

The printer can be set to run in condensed print mode by: _____
_____
_____

10 You may achieve automatic totalling of numerical fields by: _____
_____
_____

Chapter 4 – Transparency sequence 1

The distinction between program-centred and data-centred information systems and a simple definition of a database

Notes

Transparency reference

4.1.1 This poses the questions to be answered in this sequence.

4.1.2 BIRTHDAY.BAS in the student text is a very simple example of program-centred data processing since there is only one program using a single data file under the control of a single user.

In the multi-user situation, whether with micro, mini or mainframe computers, complications rapidly arise because of the kind of situation illustrated by this transparency. Users access more than one program, but this is no problem; the difficulty lies in multiple programs making calls on common files. The revision of one program may imply changes in file structure which then have repercussions on all other programs calling on that file. This is why in many large organizations, much of the programming effort is directed towards maintenance of existing software rather than the development of new programs.

Furthermore, there is commonly duplication of data. The transparency shows duplication of data items H, K and L. Apart from the unnecessary inputting effort, there is an opportunity for discrepancies to arise between one user's version of this data and another's. There is also twice the maintenance effort when the data changes.

4.1.3 The database approach to the same set of data is illustrated. Users still access more than one program, but now the data is 'isolated' from the programs by the DBMS. Changes in a program have no effect on the data; and data is entered into the database only once.

4.1.4 This emphasizes the isolation of data from the processes to be performed on it, and provides a definition of a database management system which is adequate at this level.

4.1.5 The comparison made in the foregoing transparencies and in the student text, between program-centred and data-centred approaches to data processing is summarized.

4.1.6 and 4.1.7 appear on one page in this manual and will need photocopying individually before being made into transparencies.

4.1.6 The definition of a database is taken rather further than the opening pages of Chapter 4 in the student text, and is, perhaps, not suitable for all student groups if used in a more detailed way.

Consider data relationships. All the work in the student text implies a database relating to a single entity, so the concept of related data items is simple. But in business life, databases are rarely so simple.

Take, for example, the oversimplified case of a garage keeping records of its repair/servicing activities by means of a database management system. There would be at least four entities each with their own attributes, as shown overleaf:

Customer: (name, address, telephone no. etc.)
Car: (make, model, registration no. etc.)
Repair: (date, description, parts used, etc.)
Mechanic: (name, address, tel. no., staff no., hourly rate etc.)

All the data is linked and properly belongs in one database, but there is no *direct* relationship between, say, attributes of the entity Customer and the entity Mechanic.

The final point on the transparency is that a database may consist of more than one data file. The garage example illustrates this, because data associated with each of the four entities would be kept in different files.

4.1.7 The contents of a data file are described and the terms *attribute*, *entity*, *field*, *field names*, *records* are defined. The last three terms may be illustrated if Sequence 4.3 is used (Obtaining information from data).

Chapter 4 – Transparency sequence 2
The nature of data – quantitative and qualitative

Notes

Transparency reference

4.2.1 A data tuple is presented and an analysis of the time aspect of it is made.

4.2.2 This illustrates that property values may be *absolute* or *relative* to some other value; strictly quantitative or a qualitative assessment categorized into one of a range of quanta.

4.2.3 A transparency addressing the main problems associated with the quantification of a qualitative assessment. The distinction is made between precision and accuracy, and the problem of 'middle of the road' bias is highlighted.

4.2.4 The problem of imprecision introduced in 4.2.3 is taken further by considering the implications of expressing a continuum of views in terms of only four quanta.

4.2.5 This transparency shows that imprecise data can be used as a basis for drawing valid conclusions in certain circumstances, and it includes an example of the valid use of imprecise data.

Chapter 4 – Transparency sequence 3
Obtaining information from data.
Definitions of fields and records

Notes

Transparency reference

4.3.1a We start from the standpoint of the Telephone Manager, whose prime concern is the Exchange Lines. He needs to know to whom the lines are currently leased, the equipment connected to them, etc.

4.3.1b These overlays facilitate an explanation of the terms *field*,
and c   *field name* and *record*.

4.3.2a All the *data* required for a telephone directory is available in a table of the kind illustrated in 4.3.1. But it does not give the *information* a user wants. When students are asked what processes need to be performed on the data in order to get directory information from it, they invariably go for the key issue and ask for sorting on the Customer Name field. In anticipating of that response, 4.3.2a reproduces a sorted version of 4.3.1a.

4.3.2b This overlay could be omitted, because in terms of information retrieval it has no function. However, it is desirable if one wishes to simulate a telephone directory entry accurately. It is British Telecom's style to omit the town name from the address if it is the same as the exchange name. But this aside, it may be your first opportunity, within the context of the book, to introduce conditional statements which are of such great importance in many aspects of IT.

4.3.3 This completes the job by rearranging the order in which the fields are presented – something which can be achieved under almost any database software.

4.3.4 and 4.3.5 appear on one page in this manual and will need photocopying individually before being made into transparencies.

4.3.4 The illustration is now summarized in slightly more formal terms and the significance of *key fields* is shown. In the case of the telephone directory, CUSTOMER NAME is the key field.

4.3.5 This reinforces the point that in simple cases, records are held in key order.

1 What is a database?

2 How does it differ from a program-centred information system?

3 Of what advantage is a data-centred approach?

Program-centred Data Processing (d.p.)

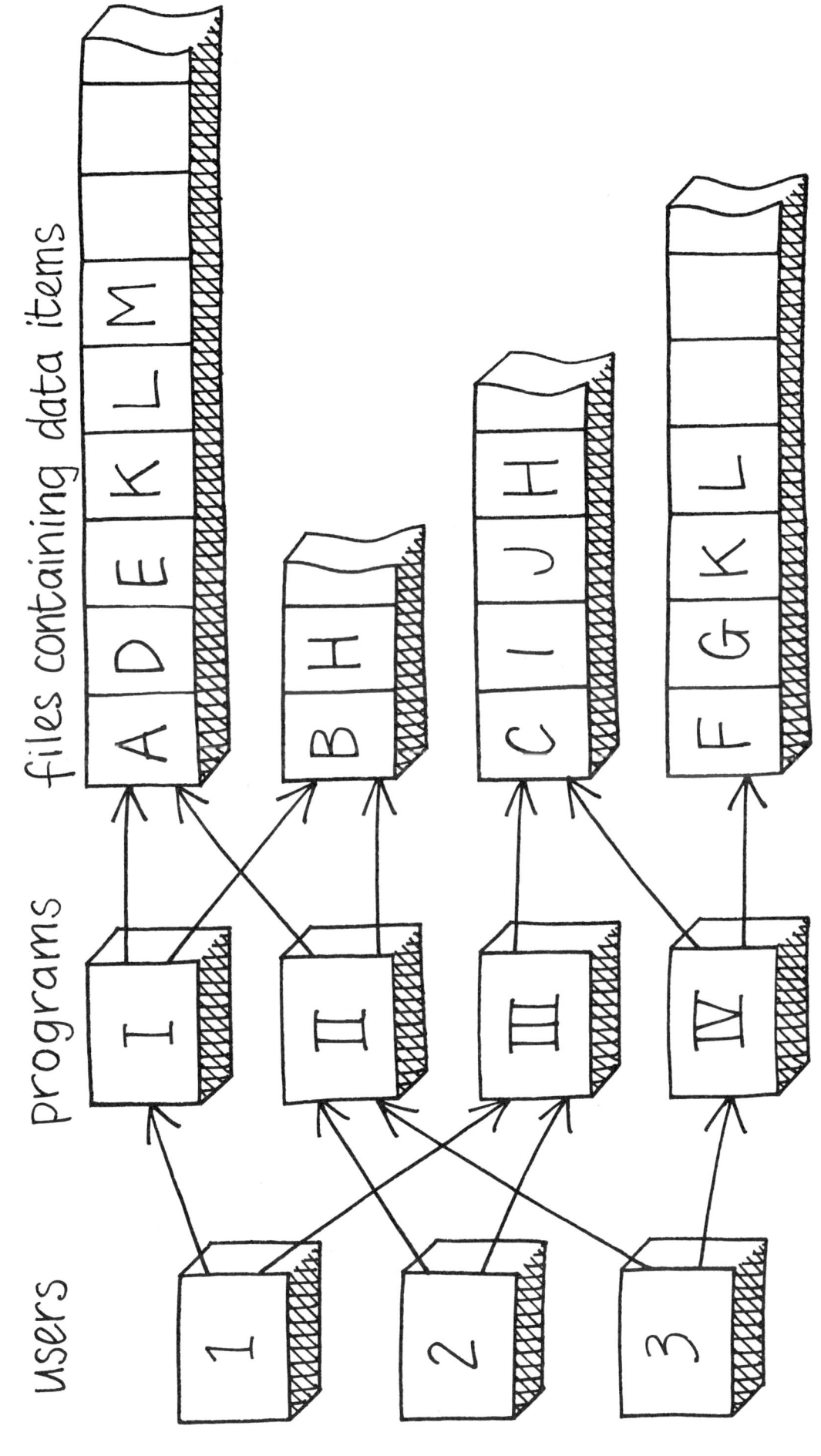

Data-centred Data Processing (d.p.)

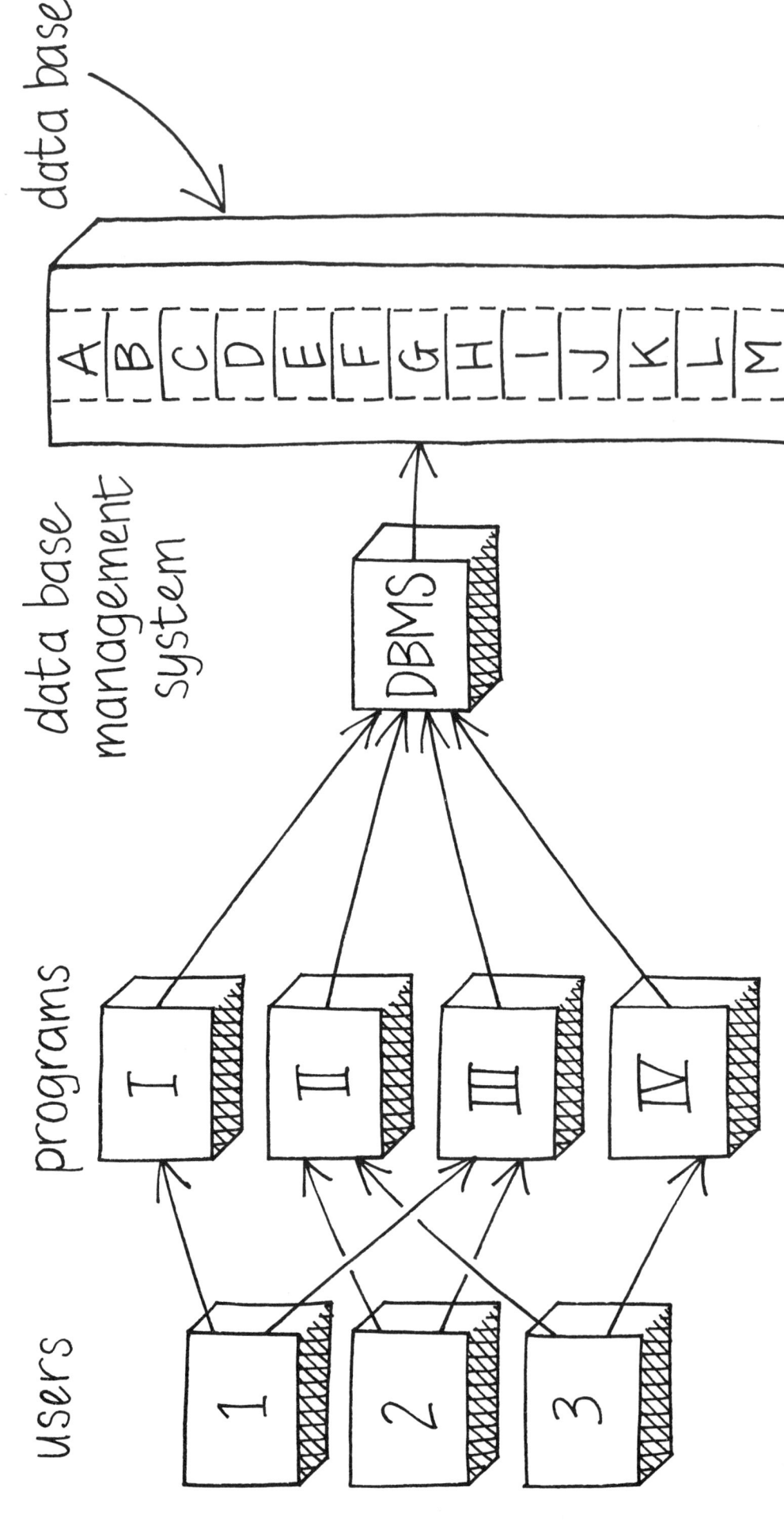

Database Management System (DBMS)

A DBMS allows retrieval and maintenance of data in a way which is meaningful (and using processes which are transparent) to the user.

This implies . . .
the definition of data must be separate from the definition of processes to be performed on the data.

DBMS includes software, hardware and procedures used to manage the database.

A Comparison of the Two Information Systems

Program-centred

Inflexible

Modifications may affect other programs

Changes are costly and time-consuming

Software written for one specific task

Data-centred

Very flexible

Data isolated from the processes performed on it

Changes easily and quickly implemented

Software is independent of specific applications and therefore useable for many different tasks

Database

A database is more than just a collection of data

It implies . . .
   that data items are related in terms
     of subject matter
   that data can be retrieved and
     viewed in more than one way

It may consist of more than one
     data file

Data File

A data file comprises a number of items of data (attributes) concerning a particular object of interest (entity)

Items of data are contained in **FIELDS** which are identified by **FIELD NAMES**

RECORDS comprise groups of relevant attributes for specific occurrences of the entity

The Nature of Data

A data tuple comprises:

object name	Smith, Arthur
object property	Age
property value	47
time	1983, May 16

We may be more interested in the relative time of phenomena than in the real time of occurrence – this information may be captured simply from the ordering of the phenomena.

Property Values

These may be absolute e.g. Age = 47

They may be relative

e.g. this lecture is very interesting
extremely boring

Essentially there must be quantification

Problems associated with quantification

How many steps? Fewer steps imply less precision Degree of precision cannot exceed accuracy of measurement (accuracy relates to the repeatability of a particular measurement)

Be aware of '**middle of the road' bias** – tend to avoid an odd number of steps.

An illustration of imprecision associated with quantification

Suppose perceptions of this lecture are quantified into four categories:

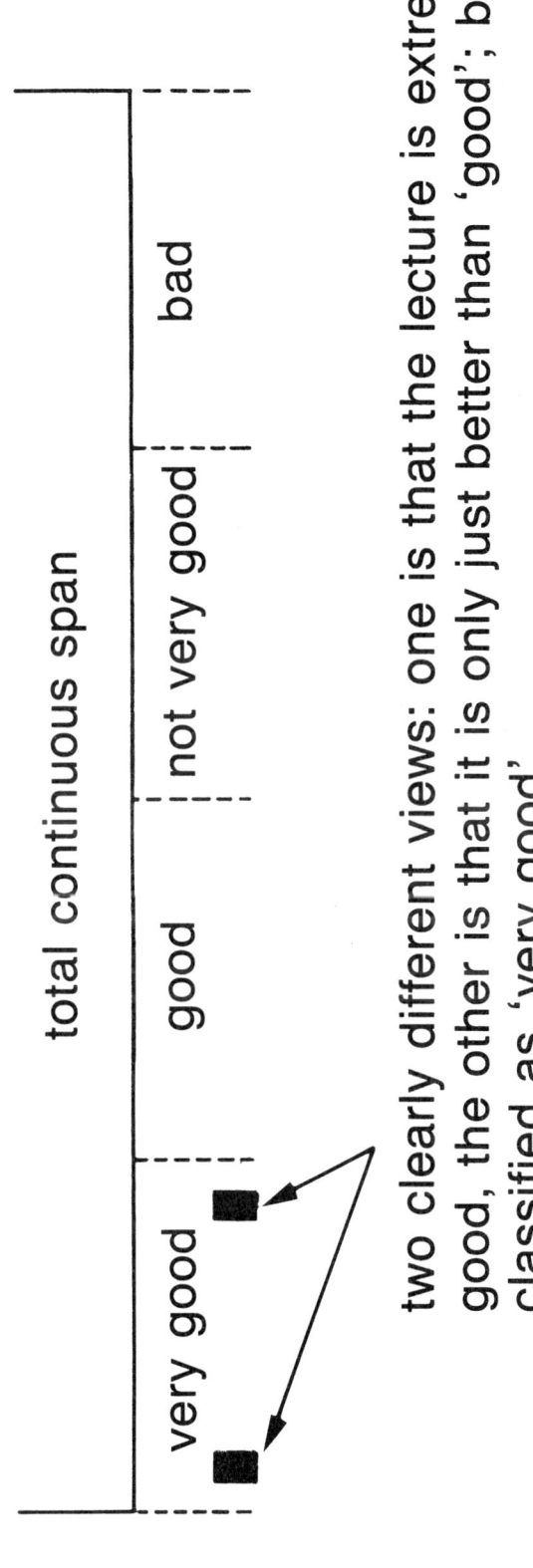

two clearly different views: one is that the lecture is extremely good, the other is that it is only just better than 'good'; both are classified as 'very good'

The use of imprecise data

This is valid if:

conclusions are not drawn in respect of individual data items

decisions arising from the use of the data are based on a degree of imprecision not less than that involved in categorizing the data

for example:

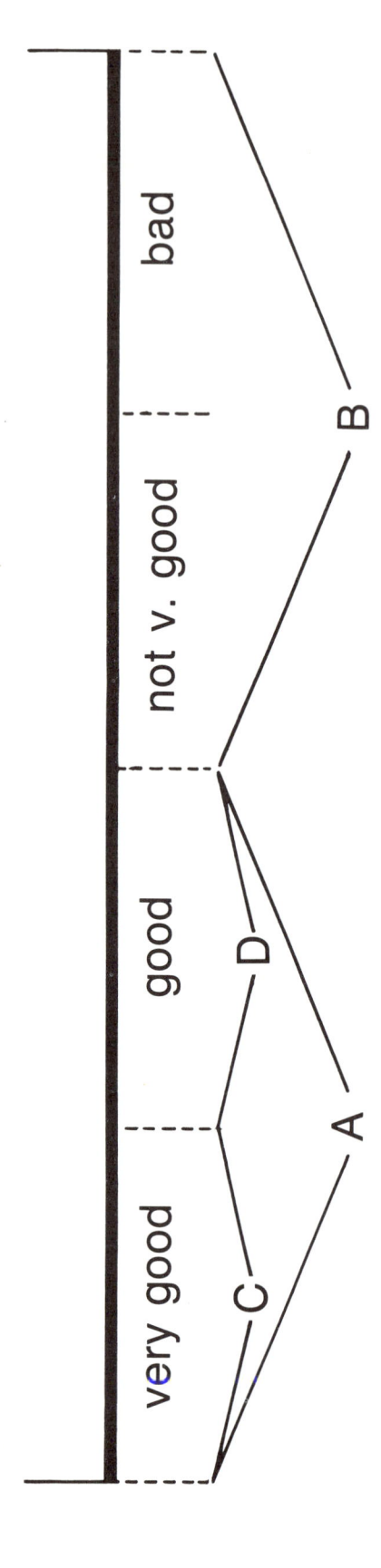

If A>B, use lecturer again; if A≤B, find somebody else

If C≥D, increase lecturer's programme

Information from Data 1

Consider data concerning customers held by British Telecom

Exchange name	Allocated tel no	Customer name	Address line 1	Address line 2	Address ...etc
Oxford	50000	Smith A J	2 High St	Oxford	
Oxford	50001	Jones R	5 Wells Rd	Botley	
Oxford	50002				
Oxford	50003	Brown B	7 Pear La	Cowley	
Oxford	50004	Green C	4 River Cl	Oxford	
etc	etc	etc	etc	etc	

4.3.1b

Field →

Field

Field names

Record ↑

Information from Data 2

Reorganization of data for directory entries – stage 1

Exchange name	Allocated tel no	Customer name	Address line 1	Address line 2	. . . etc
Oxford	50003	Brown B	7 Pear La	Cowley	
Oxford	50004	Green C	4 River Cl	Oxford	
Oxford	50001	Jones R	5 Wells Rd	Botley	
Oxford	50000	Smith A J	2 High St	Oxford	

Alphabetic sort on field 'Customer name'

+ stage 2

Selection and processing on criteria specified for field 'Address line 2' e.g. IF Address line 2 = "Oxford" THEN Address line 2 = " "

Information from Data 3

Reorganization of data for directory entries – stage 3

Customer name	Address line 1	Address line 2	Exchange name	Allocated tel no
Brown B	7 Pear La	Cowley	Oxford	50003
Green C	4 River Cl		Oxford	50004
Jones R	5 Wells Rd	Botley	Oxford	50001
Smith A J	2 High St		Oxford	50000

The order in which the data fields are presented for output has been changed

Getting Information from Data

To *use* data (i.e. to get information from it), you must be able to retrieve it in the form you want to look at it.

Retrieval:

One or more data item(s) in each record must act as a **KEY** . . .

If you know the value of the **KEY FIELD(S)** you can identify the values of all attributes for that particular record of the entity.

The KEY must be easily located.

In the simplest cases, records are sorted in key order (e.g. telephone directories).

CHAPTER 5　First steps in word processing

In this chapter we stress that accuracy when inputting is vitally important. It is very easy to fall into bad habits when correction is so easy to perform. However, word processors should not be regarded as aids for lazy typists. When properly used, they are tools for increased productivity. To avoid wastage of materials, students should be actively discouraged from adopting a 'print first and check later' attitude. They must check their work on screen before printing. The ease of correction and reprinting has undoubtedly led to time wasting, and typists are not solely to blame. Authors too try to perfect their work with repeated drafts.

Printed output is familiar media to students, but how many of them have looked closely at printed output and noticed not only the differences in character size and line spacing, but also character shape (*fonts*)? We have moved quickly over the last few years from either having letter quality, or not, to being able to choose different fonts and point sizes, incorporating graphics. The advent of desk-top publishing has revolutionized the type of printed output we may have. Transparency sequence 5.1 indicates some of these possiblities.

Saving text and recalling it may serve more than one purpose. The most obvious one is that text typed as a draft will need to be corrected or altered and recalling the draft version for editing will save a complete retype.

Recalling text in the form of standard letters, other documents or just paragraphs and reusing them for different purposes, may not be so obvious.

Standard paragraphs may be reused to form documents, a process known as *boilerplating*. Lawyers, for example, might use clauses that have been tried and tested in court (known as 'precedents') to compile wills or contracts. Transparency sequence 5.2 may help students to understand what is meant by *boilerplating* and also sets out the advantages of using prerecorded text.

Standard letters can be used to deal with a large number of correspondence matters in an office. It might be a useful exercise for students new to the concept, to identify the sort of standard letters that might be used, say, in a Personnel Department, i.e. letters calling candidates to interview, letters of rejection, letters of appointment, etc. (Students could be asked to write such letters and identify the variable information, to reinforce the concept of 'standard' text and 'variable' text.) Standard letters are most probably encountered by students when they are on the receiving end of a *mailshot* i.e. a sales drive by letter. Transparency sequence 5.3 offers an example of the mailshot standard letter technique.

The flexibility of text once it has been word processed is another important concept and we have supplied a pro forma covering basic text processing at the end of this chapter. In the student text, we try to explain the difference between editing/correcting the characters and improving the appearance by using different page formats in terms of character size, line spacing, justification etc. Recognition of different text formats will be aided by referring to the single transparency, 5.4. When encouraging students to proof-read, particularly longer documents with multiple levels of headings and indents, it might be useful for them to regard checking the spelling as a different process to checking the format. It means they would have to look at documents twice, but for younger people it is often better for them to do one thing at a time and do it well, than to lose concentration by trying to remember too many things at once. Gradually, of course, this dual-reading technique could be replaced by a single comprehensive reading.

One should also point out that word processing is not the panacea to all typing tasks in an office environment. The completion of official documentation and forms generated elsewhere is best done on a typewriter as trying to line-up on a screen-based system wastes too much time for the one-off job. (It might be helpful to have sample forms on hand, such as export documentation, company annual returns, etc., when introducing this point to students.) Equally *ad hoc* jobs, such as the occasional envelope, can be done faster with a typewriter than with a word processing system. (You could ask one of your students to produce an envelope using word processing and one using the typewriter and time them.)

Ergonomic considerations as illustrated in Transparency sequence 5.5 have been dealt with at greater length in this chapter than elsewhere in the student text. But the points we raise here apply to all VDU users. Keyboard construction may not be an aspect of ergonomics that is often given much consideration beyond sculptured keys and sloping keyboards, since students will, in all likelihood, have little opportunity to handle any of the different keyboards other than QWERTY. But substantial amounts of study have gone into designing the layout of the Dvořák and Maltron (see Transparency 5.5) from the point of view of operator comfort and improved accuracy. After all, ergonomics is essentially the study of improving the working environment so as to increase operator efficiency (from the Greek: *ergon*, work).

Buying a full-blown computer system with word processing was once an expensive outlay for very small businesses and many typewriter manufacturers offered a step-by-step approach to building a word processing system from an electronic typewriter. (Some still do, and systems built this way are even beginning to claim IBM-compatibility.) Whilst this once had economic advantages, the ever decreasing price of micros now makes this a questionable option. Conversely, a printer capable of producing letter quality still seems to cost a disproportionate amount compared to the price of the computer and associated software. Using an electronic typewriter as the printer may seem attractive at first sight. However, the typewriter as printer will not stand up to the extensive use that most offices make of printing equipment driven by micros.

The discussions about the pros and cons of micro-computer-based word processing and dedicated word processors will raise less controversy today than it might have done in the early 1980s. Although many people involved in the typing field might have preferred a dedicated option, there is little competition left as market forces have chosen the cheaper and more flexible micro-based option, which allows other applications to run on the same machine.

There has been heated discussion about page-based vs. document-based systems, and command vs. menu-driven systems; often it is a matter of personal choice and/or the type of work being undertaken. By *page*, we do not necessarily mean an A4-sized page, but rather a unit of perhaps 90 lines which would need to be saved before further typing could be done. Document-based systems would handle as much text as the RAM could hold, and text flows freely from page-to-page as insertions and deletions are made. Typically, one might be able to handle files which are the equivalent of 20 A4 pages, before the system starts to slow down noticeably, as it tries to off-load some text out of RAM to make room for further typing.

A systematic approach to file naming is as essential as file references for a manual filing system (see Chapter 2 of the student text). It is also necessary to keep a record of the files on a disk so that colleagues (or fellow-students) know how long documents should be kept before they are deleted, or can check to see when the last back-up disk was made. The single transparency, 5.6, may be useful in explaining this. Students should be encouraged to keep up-to-date records of their disks and to make regular back-up copies . Guidance on printing and sorting file information kept by the operating system is given in Chapter 2 of the student text.

Most of the practical exercises in the Pupil's Book deal with text editing before moving on to print enhancements, and are, in our opinion, best done rather than discussed. So there is little in the way of additional support material in this chapter. It may be, however, that students encounter some difficulty in using the BSI proof-correction symbols if they are not already familiar with them. The BSI symbols are appended to the student text, but if practice in proof-reading skills is required, we have included a couple of exercises as items II and III in Appendix 2 which may be of use.

The one area where further formal input will almost certainly be required is the calculation of printing positions. When printed on headed stationery, one has to avoid logos at the head or left-hand margin of the page, or may have to line up the printing to coincide with Our Ref, Date, or Extension headings. Precise line-up is also necessary if one uses window envelopes. Line length is also important, and depending on the software being used, it may be defined in terms of margins which are set to so many characters. In such cases, students are immediately faced with calculations involving pitch; worse still, pitch is invariably related to inches – a somewhat unfamiliar unit to present-day school-leavers. The transparencies in Sequence 5.7 may help to overcome these difficulties.

It would be valuable for students to type a short letter and then practise lining up their printing for different types of blank stationery e.g. College notepaper (or photocopies of it, if it is too precious!)

Transparency sequence 5.7 provides the basic data for conversion from metric to imperial for the large number of word processing systems that still work in imperial, and also gives information about paper sizes (the A sizes being in metric). Additionally, we supply a grid as item IV in Appendix 2, which could be photocopied for students. The grid can be held up to the light behind different types of stationery, so that students can see how many lines down or how many character positions they would need to move across, to line up their printing accurately.

Be warned when photocopying the master copy of the grid, however. Some photocopiers may distort the rulings slightly, so do check for accurate reproduction before assuming that it is safe to use. If you discover that the distortion is too great, then you could ask students to design their own.

Dealing with the setting of left- and right-margins will depend very much on the system you are using. With WordStar, setting the margins on screen may result in the text appearing half on and half off the screen if the menu options are used. If your system produces something similar, then it would be better to introduce an *offset* command which shifts the printing of the page over by a specified number of characters at print time (with WordStar, one would use the embedded command .po and the required number of characters).

Control over paper lengths could also be used to produce labels, for example. Labels are in fact very short pages of, say, 9 lines (if the labels measure 1.5 inches from the top of one to the top of the next) with no room for blank lines at the top and perhaps only one or two at the bottom to prevent typing printing in the gap between one label and the next.

Pagination facilities will differ between systems, but students should be encouraged to keep an eye open for *widows* and *orphans* (defined in Transparency 5.8) and know how to use pagination or forced page breaks to avoid the occurrence of either. The final exercise in this chapter of the Pupil's Book allows the student to deal with documents longer than a single page and should raise the question of where to place page breaks.

This final exercise also introduces the use of copied blocks – the objective being to encourage the student to look for short cuts by reusing text whenever possible.

The use of *search-and-replace* as an editing tool is also shown in this exercise. It would be possible to extend the use of this feature to type frequently used phrases or words and so to regard it as also a production tool. Students could be given a small telephone directory to type. Frequently used exchange names could be coded, using combinations of characters that are unlikely to be used elsewhere (such as LND for London). Using an *exact* search-and-replace would cut down repeated typing, speed up an otherwise boring job and avoid the introduction of errors.

In all the practical wordprocessing work we have suggested students may find helpful a concise listing of keystrokes necessary to perform the required operations. Such a listing is provided for WordStar on the pages that follow. We have also included a *pro forma* which you can complete and photocopy for the word-processing software available to your students.

First steps in word processing

Your WP software is called:	WordStar
	Command
Command file containing your word processing software is:	WS.COM
To open an existing document file for editing:	D + file name
To begin a new document:	D + file name
To enter text:	Simply type the text, but do not press ENTER at the end of a line unless you intend to end a paragraph or leave a blank line
Cursor movement by character or by line:	use 'arrow' keys
Cursor movement – by word right: by word left:	CTRL + F CTRL + A
Cursor movement down a screenful at a time:	use PG DN
Cursor movement up a screenful at a time:	use PG UP
To save work you have typed: (so that you can print it)	CTRL + K + D
To abandon any changes made to a file:	CTRL + K + Q
To print: (from opening menu)	P + file name + either ESC – to avoid subsequent print options if not needed or ENTER – to answer questions about print options
To insert a character/characters:	INSERT mode is ON by default, place cursor on the character to be moved aside and type the missing text
To overtype an incorrect character:	Turn INSERT off by CTRL + V or use INS key
To reform corrected text:	CTRL + B for each paragraph (watch screen prompts if hyphen-help is offered)

To erase an incorrect character you have just typed:	DEL key
To erase an incorrect character immediately under the cursor:	CTRL + G
To delete a word:	CTRL + T
To delete a line:	CTRL + Y
To delete a block of text:	CTRL + K + B to define the beginning of a block Move cursor to end of block CTRL + K + K to define the end of a block CTRL + K + Y to delete the block
To copy a block of text:	CTRL + K + B to define the beginning of a block Move cursor to end of block CTRL + K + K to define the end of a block Move cursor to destination CTRL + K + C to copy the block
To move a block of text:	CTRL + K + B to define the beginning of a block Move cursor to end of block CTRL + K + K to define the end of a block Move cursor to destination CTRL + K + V to move the block
To remove the highlighting after block operations:	CTRL + K + H
To justify text:	Ensure that justify is ON CTRL + O to check the onscreen menu, J to turn justify ON, if it is OFF; reform text if necessary
To remove justification:	Ensure that justify is OFF CTRL + O to check the Onscreen Menu, J to turn justify ON, if it is OFF; reform text if necessary
To centre text:	Type the heading, then CTRL + O + C
To underline text:	CTRL + P + S to begin underlining, CTRL + P + S to end (displays codes on screen)
To embolden text:	CTRL + P + B to begin emboldening, CTRL + P + B to end (displays codes on screen)
To set right margin:	CTRL + O + R + column number required
To set left margin:	Either CTRL + O + L + column number required, or .po + number of columns required for the offset

To set tabs: (left-hand tabs)	CTRL + O + I + column number required
To set tabs that will line up over the decimal point:	CTRL + O + I + # + column number required
To clear a single tab:	CTRL + O + N + column number of tab to be cleared
To clear all tabs:	CTRL + O + N + A
To search-and-replace text:	CTRL + Q + A, type text to be found, ENTER, type replacement text, ENTER, type ? + ENTER for options, type character(s) representing the option(s) required, ENTER
To set paper lengths:	.pl + number of lines
To set the margin to be left at top of every page before first line of typing:	.mt + number of lines
To set the margin to be left at bottom of every page after last line of typing:	.mb + number of lines (note: must be at least 2 lines if page numbers ON)
To turn off page numbering:	.op
To force a page break:	.pa

First steps in word processing

Your WP software is called: _____

	Command
Command file containing your word processing software is:	
To open an existing document file for editing:	
To begin a new document:	
To enter text:	
Cursor movement by character or by line:	
Cursor movement – by word right: by word left:	
Cursor movement down a screenful at a time:	
Cursor movement up a screenful at a time:	

To save work you have typed: (so that you can print it)	
To abandon any changes made to a file:	
To print:	
To insert a character/characters:	
To overtype an incorrect character:	
To reform corrected text:	
To erase an incorrect character you have just typed:	
To erase an incorrect character immediately under the cursor:	
To delete a word:	
To delete a line:	
To delete a block of text:	
To copy a block of text:	
To move a block of text:	
To remove the highlighting after block operations:	
To justify text:	

To remove justification:

To centre text:

To underline text:

To embolden text:

To set right margins:

To set left margins:

To set tabs:
(left-hand tabs)

To set tabs that will line up over the decimal point:

To clear a single tab:

To clear all tabs:

To search-and-replace text:

To set paper lengths:

To set the margin to be left at top of every page before first line of typing:

To set the margin to be left at bottom of every page after last line of typing:

To turn off page numbering:

To force a page break:

Chapter 5 – Transparency sequence 1
Text enhancement and font choices

Notes

Transparency reference

5.1.1 and 5.1.2 appear on one page in this manual and will need photocopying individually before being made into transparencies.

5.1.1 This exemplifies very basic print enhancement features commonly found on printers.

5.1.2 An illustration of features that are found on most matrix printers, but *not* on daisy-wheel or golf-ball printers. This transparency emphasizes the flexibility of printers which generate characters from dot patterns.

5.1.3 This shows some fonts and the variation of point sizes available with laser printers. The examples are taken from Hewlett Packard Laserjet fonts. The first eight will display well using an OHP; the remainder will not be easily readable, but are included to give some impression of the considerable range of point sizes available even with a middle-of-the-range laser printer.

Chapter 5 – Transparency sequence 2
Boilerplating

Notes

Transparency reference

5.2.1 A definition of 'boilerplating', together with an example of this technique.

The standard paragraphs are kept to one side of the transparency so that you may write on a clear overlay on the left. One might describe several different scenarios and seek student views on which paragraphs to select. It seems to us that possible combinations could include:

    1 and a closing block
    1,2 and a closing block
    1,3 and a closing block
    1,2,4 and a closing block
    1,3,4 and a closing block

There is an opportunity for integration with English studies, for example, here in the use of collective nouns. 'Literature' at the end of paragraph 1 is satisfactory, but 'brochure' would not have been because its singular and plural forms differ and potential buyers may be interested in single products or more than one product.

Students could be encouraged to design standard paragraphs to meet a range of situations in a given context.

5.2.2 This indicates some of the uses to which boilerplating can be put.

5.2.3 An explanation of the advantages of boilerplating standard text which also indicates a possible limitation. Depending on the extent of modification required, it may still be worth using a standard paragraph and editing it on-screen.

Chapter 5 – Transparency sequence 3
Mailshots

Notes

Transparency reference

5.3a This is the basic letter which everyone on our 'customer' list is going to receive; gaps have been left where the variable information is to be inserted.

5.3b An overlay supplying one set of variable data which fits into the gaps. The question then is: how can we put something in the gaps which will represent the variable data for *any* record in our customer list?

5.3c This overlay substitutes for 5.3b and is relevant only for WordStar users. Its inclusion here is simply to offer an idea for a possible approach to the introduction of variable names and the linking of them to the structure of the mailing list file.

Chapter 5 – Transparency 4
Text formatting

There is only one transparency in this sequence. It illustrates, in *outline* shape, a number of different text formats. The uses generally made of each for draft and formal documents, etc. are explained in the student text. They need no further comment, other than to remark that some people refer to the *non-justified* format as *left flush*.

Chapter 5 – Transparency sequence 5
Ergonomic considerations

Notes

Transparency reference

5.5.1 These diagrams indicate some possible equipment layouts that could be used to help operators achieve comfortable working positions.

Students should consider suitable posture to avoid strain, when using computing equipment for prolonged periods.

5.5.2 This shows a satisfactory range of sitting positions and also refers to correct working height by implication, in that it commends working without undue bending of the wrist.

5.5.3 Well-positioned copy holders are very useful in avoiding neck strain. In the small inset picture on this transparency, we see that there is virtually no need for head movement – the eyes can move in a vertical line from the copy to the screen and back again.

5.5.4 Glare on screens is a particular problem if VDUs are badly sited or overhead lighting is not well designed. These aspects of ambient light must be taken into consideration. This transparency tackles some aspects of the problem. Overhead lighting, that is diffused so that the whole area is uniformly lit without any glare, is ideal.

If glare is unavoidable, then gauze screens, or screens which reduce glare by polarizing the light passing through them, can be purchased to fix in front of the offending screen.

5.5.5 The QWERTY keyboard has been with us a long time and for that reason alone will be difficult to replace. However, a number of companies have attempted to redesign the key layout and have made extensive studies of the best design to reduce typing errors. The Dvorak keyboard is featured in the student text, but this is a picture of the Maltron keyboard. Notice the 'dished' construction as well as clearly separated key-pads.

Chapter 5 – Transparency 6
Disk catalogues

At this stage students should be well aware of the use of DIR as the internal command to display on screen the directory information for a specified path. They may not have taken much notice of the data beyond the file name and extension, and this may be the time to point out the value of the additional data – the file size, to give an idea of how large a document you are dealing with, and the date/time stamp so that you can be sure when it was last amended.

Students may be less familiar about obtaining a hard copy output of this directory information. This may be the opportunity to go through the command DIR [path]>PRN with them. (An MSDOS/PCDOS operating system is assumed here.) If you have the system utility SORT.EXE available, you could extend the command to DIR [path]|SORT>PRN with students where appropriate. But a copy of the directory information, sorted or not, is insufficient for a proper disk catalogue. We need to add some text to indicate the general content of the file, the date up to which it should not be removed from disk, and directions regarding archiving if appropriate.

Students practising this might be satisfied with just producing a hard copy of the directory information and then handwriting the remaining detail alongside. But a more professional approach would be to save the sorted directory information to a file and then import that ASCII file under appropriate software to add the further comment and deletion date information. This could be done under word processing software, but more usefully it might be done under database software. Then files due to be deleted could be chosen readily, by selecting on appropriate date criteria.

Chapter 5 – Transparency sequence 7
Print positions, pitch and paper sizes

Notes

Transparency reference		
	5.7.1a	This transparency is drawn to scale, so that six lines occupy the same space as ten characters in 10-pitch and twelve characters in 12-pitch. It is dimensioned to show the equivalence of 1 inch and 25.4 mm (note that millimetres are used in preference to centimetres since this is standard industrial practice) and it also introduces the symbol ″ to represent the word 'inch(es)'. It will be of particular value if your students are using a word processing system which dimensions margins in characters rather than absolute measurements. You may wish to overlay it with a blank transparency and then write appropriate text over it to make a particular point. By way of example:
	5.7.1b	This is an overlay which carries text in both 10-pitch and 12-pitch and makes reference to margin calculations.
	5.7.2	This transparency shows the dimensions of standard A sizes of paper from A3 down to A6. By placing the dotted diagonal line across them, we endeavour to show that they all have exactly the same aspect ratio, i.e. their sides are always in the same proportion.
	5.7.3	This shows the aspect ratio to be 1:2 and also shows how sheets with successive A numbers have exactly half the area of the next larger sheet. Should you wish to broaden the syllabus at this point, the transparency does provide an opportunity to talk about paper weights, since weights are given in grammes per square metre, (a m^2 being the size of an A0 sheet).

Chapter 5 – Transparency sequence 8
Widows and orphans

This provides a straightforward illustration of widows and orphans. Whilst the obvious way to deal with either situation is to use a forced page break, it may be worthwhile pointing out that if one is working on a relatively short, say 2- or 3-page document, an orphan on the last page may sometimes better be avoided by quite minor marginal changes throughout the whole document than by using a forced page break.

Print Enhancement

Nearly all printers offer some print enhancement facilities.

The most commonly found are **emboldening** and <u>underlining</u>, either separately or **<u>together</u>**

With matrix printers . . .

condensed, elongated and *italic* styles are usually available.

These effects are produced by **control codes** sent by the software to the printer. They can be applied to most fonts.

Portrait Fonts

FONT ID	NAME	PITCH	POINT SIZE	SYMBOL SET	PRINT SAMPLE
\'PERMANENT\' SOFT FONTS					
S01	BC*140B BOLD	PS	13.9	0U	ABCDEfghij#$@[\]^`{|}~123
S02	BC*180B BOLD	PS	18	0U	ABCDEfghij#$@[\]^`{|}~1
S03	BC*240B BOLD	PS	24	0U	ABCDEfghij#$@[\]^`
S04	BC*300B BOLD	PS	29.8	0U	ABCDEfghij#$@[
S05	RB*140I ITALIC	PS	13.9	0U	ABCDEfghij#$@[\]^`{|}~123
S06	RB*180I ITALIC	PS	18	0U	ABCDEfghij#$@[\]^`{|}~1
S07	RB*240I ITALIC	PS	24	0U	ABCDEfghij#$@[\]^`
S08	RB*300I ITALIC	PS	29.8	0U	ABCDEfghij#$@
S09	GA*060R	PS	6	0U	ABCDEfghij#$@[\]^`{|}~123
S10	GA*060I ITALIC	PS	6	0U	ABCDEfghij#$@[\]^`{|}~123
S11	GA*060B BOLD	PS	6	0U	ABCDEfghij#$@[\]^`{|}~123
S12	GA*070R	PS	7	0U	ABCDEfghij#$@[\]^`{|}~123
S13	GA*070I ITALIC	PS	7	0U	ABCDEfghij#$@[\]^`{|}~123
S14	GA*070B BOLD	PS	7	0U	ABCDEfghij#$@[\]^`{|}~123
S15	GA*080R	PS	7.9	0U	ABCDEfghij#$@[\]^`{|}~123
S16	GA*080I ITALIC	PS	7.9	0U	ABCDEfghij#$@[\]^`{|}~123
S17	GA*080B BOLD	PS	7.9	0U	ABCDEfghij#$@[\]^`{|}~123
S18	GA*090R	PS	8.9	0U	ABCDEfghij#$@[\]^`{|}~123
S19	GA*090I ITALIC	PS	8.9	0U	ABCDEfghij#$@[\]^`{|}~123
S20	GA*090B BOLD	PS	8.9	0U	ABCDEfghij#$@[\]^`{|}~123
S21	GA*100R	PS	9.8	0U	ABCDEfghij#$@[\]^`{|}~123
S22	GA*100I ITALIC	PS	9.8	0U	ABCDEfghij#$@[\]^`{|}~123
S23	GA*100B BOLD	PS	9.8	0U	ABCDEfghij#$@[\]^`{|}~123
S24	GA*110R	PS	11	0U	ABCDEfghij#$@[\]^`{|}~123
S25	GA*110I ITALIC	PS	11	0U	ABCDEfghij#$@[\]^`{|}~123
S26	GA*110B BOLD	PS	11	0U	ABCDEfghij#$@[\]^`{|}~123
S27	GA*120R	PS	12	0U	ABCDEfghij#$@[\]^`{|}~123
S28	GA*120I ITALIC	PS	12	0U	ABCDEfghij#$@[\]^`{|}~123
S29	GA*120B BOLD	PS	12	0U	ABCDEfghij#$@[\]^`{|}~123
S30	GA*140R	PS	13.9	0U	ABCDEfghij#$@[\]^`{|}~123

Boilerplating

Boilerplating = making up documents by drawing together selected standard paragraphs.

1. Thank you for your interest in our product range; we have pleasure in enclosing appropriate literature.

2. The XYZ vacuum cleaner is one of the most powerful on the market. Its 1000W motor enables it to suck up just about anything.

3. The turbo superclean washing machine out-classes all others – even those costing nearly twice as much. It is fully automatic – just load it and start. The results are superb.

4. Don't take our word for it. Why not visit one of our stockists today to see a demonstration?

Boilerplating Applications

Documents particularly suited to boilerplating techniques include:

Legal documents
- **contracts**
- **wills**
- **deeds**

   etc

Specifications
Bills of quantity

Advantages . . .
of using pre-typed text:

1 **It will be accurate** (assuming that the original has been checked)
2 **It reduces production time**
3 **It relieves authors of unnecessary repetitive work**

Limitation . . .
of using pre-typed text:
Standard paragraphs may not be entirely appropriate in all circumstances

The Standardized Letter

Dear

Thank you for your order dated   for a

Thank you too for your cheque for £   ; a receipt is enclosed.

Your   will be despatched within a few days. We think you will be delighted with it, but should it fail to please, do not hesitate to contact us.

Yours sincerely

L A Zee
Managing Director

Mrs A Webber
27 Beech Road
Oxford

Mrs Webber

27 October

domestic robot

500.00

domestic robot

.df customer.lst
.rv title, init, name, add1, add2, ordate, etc.

&title& &init& &name
&add1&
&add2&

   &title& &name&

                  &ordate&
&appliance&

                    &sum&

   &appliance&

Text Formatting

If you were asked to type a draft document - ie a document that might undergo editing or revision by the author, you would choose double line spacing to allow room for alterations.

You might change to single line spacing once the final draft had been approved. If you wanted to highlight a quotation

>   you would alter the left and
>   right hand margins like this
>   to <u>indent</u> the text.

If the document was a formal one, you might choose to justify the text. This would make each line the same length by inserting <u>soft</u> spaces. If the document was a letter, however, justification would be inappropriate because the reader may gain the impression of it having been 'word processed' - one of many such letters.

Some Possible Computer Workstation Layouts

Ergonomic Considerations

Watch posture

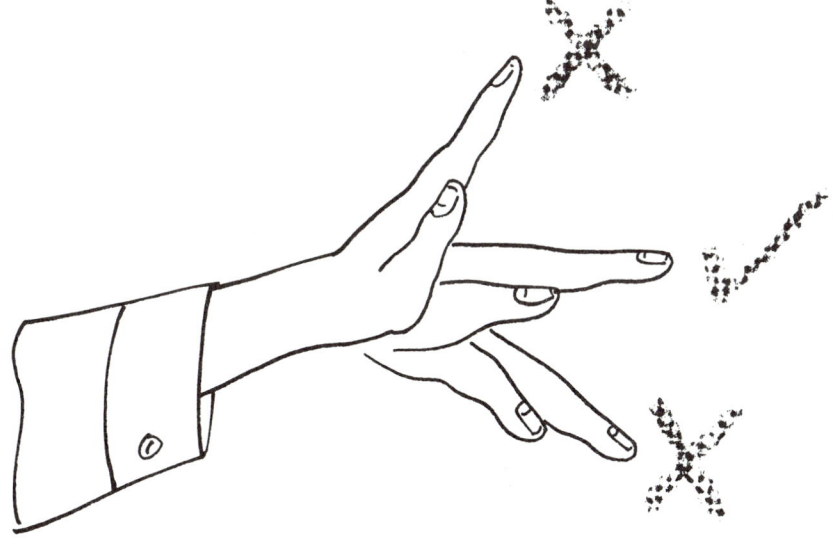

Keep wrist fairly level

Copy holders help to ensure a correct and comfortable working position. Note vertical eye movement.

Ambient Light

Try to avoid . . .
- reflections on screen
- looking directly at windows or bright lights

You may find it helpful to . . .
- tilt or turn the screen
- adjust curtains or blinds

Always adjust the VDU brightness control to suit lighting conditions.

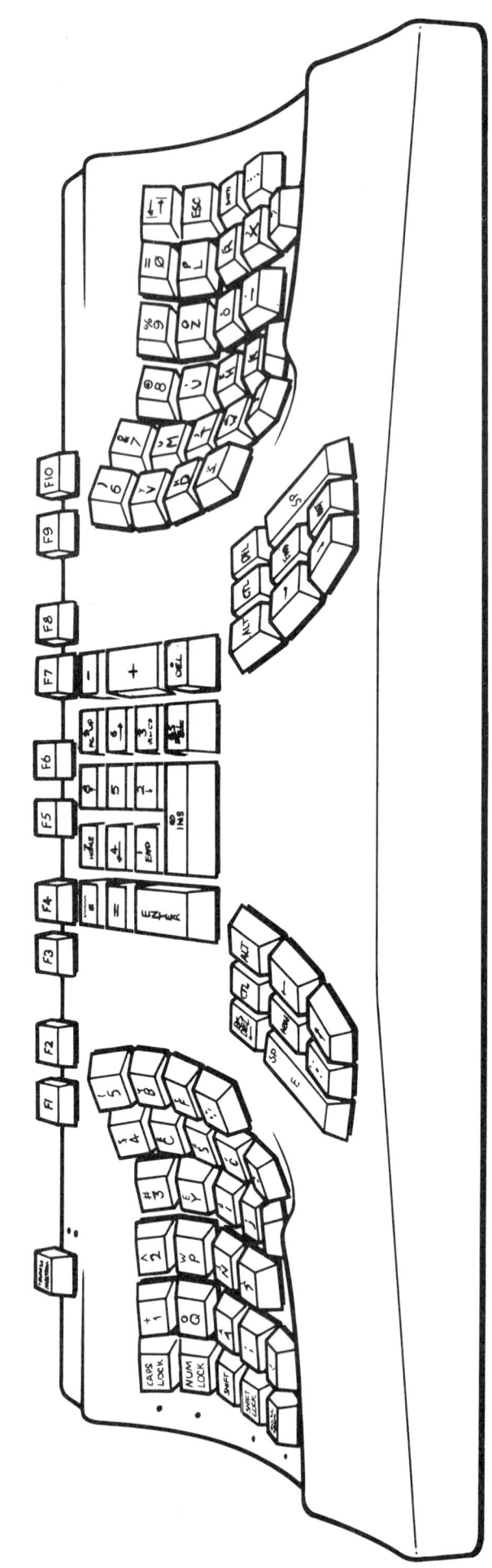

Keeping Track of Disk Contents

Example of data held on disk directory tracks and output by the **DIR** command:

A comprehensive hardcopy catalogue of disk contents should contain this information plus . . . .

1 **a brief description of what the file contains**
    (e.g. Letter to Austin Rover re. staff training)
2 **date after which it should be deleted from active disk**
3 **archive before deletion? (Y/N)**
4 (if archiving required) **the archiving medium to be used**
    (e.g. hardcopy, microfilm, magnetic media etc.)

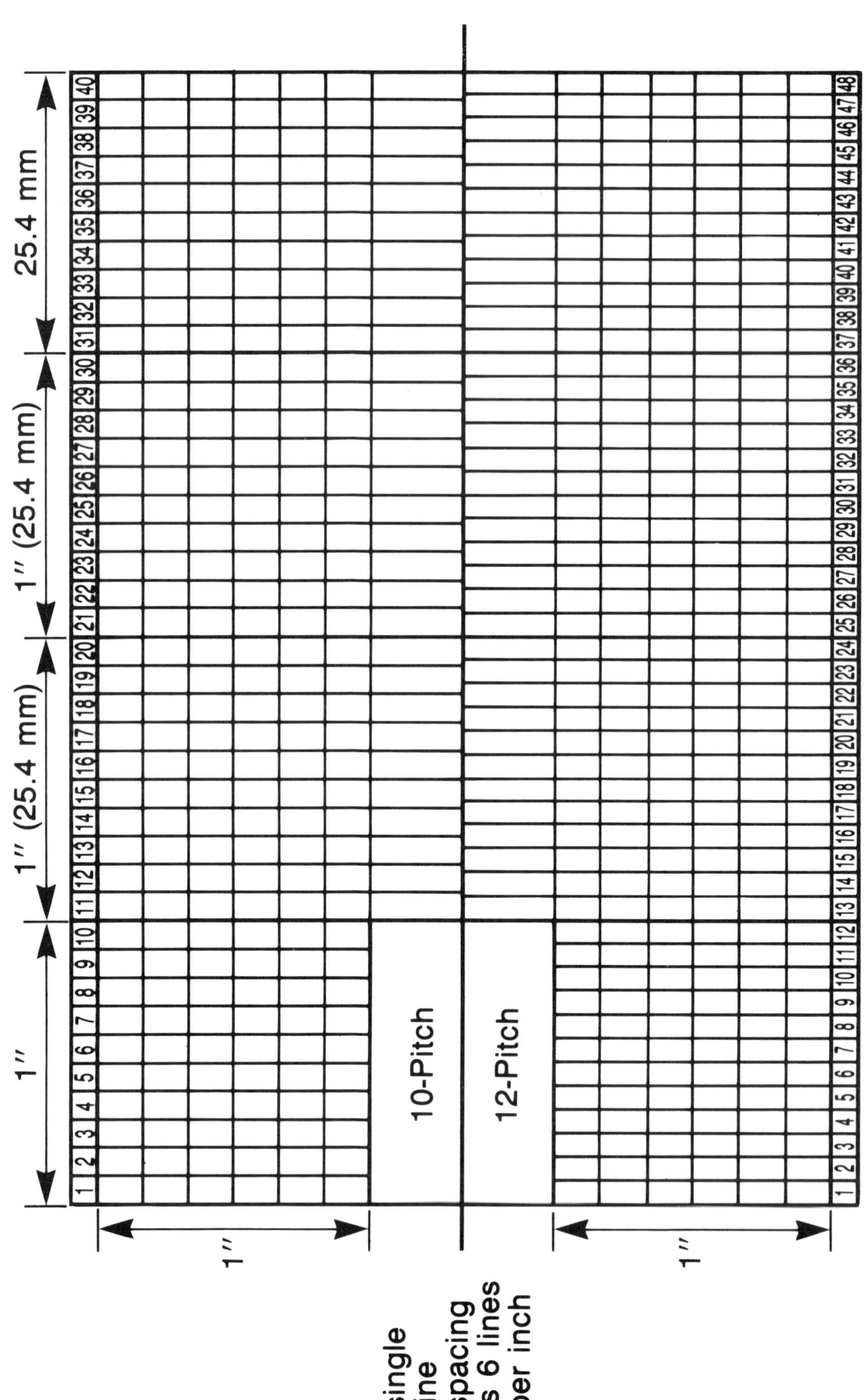

5.7.1a

With 10-pitch there are ten characters to the inch. If you want a 1" (2.5 cm) margin, start in column 11.

With 12-pitch there are twelve characters to the inch. To obtain a 1 inch margin, start in column 13.

Standard Paper Sizes 1

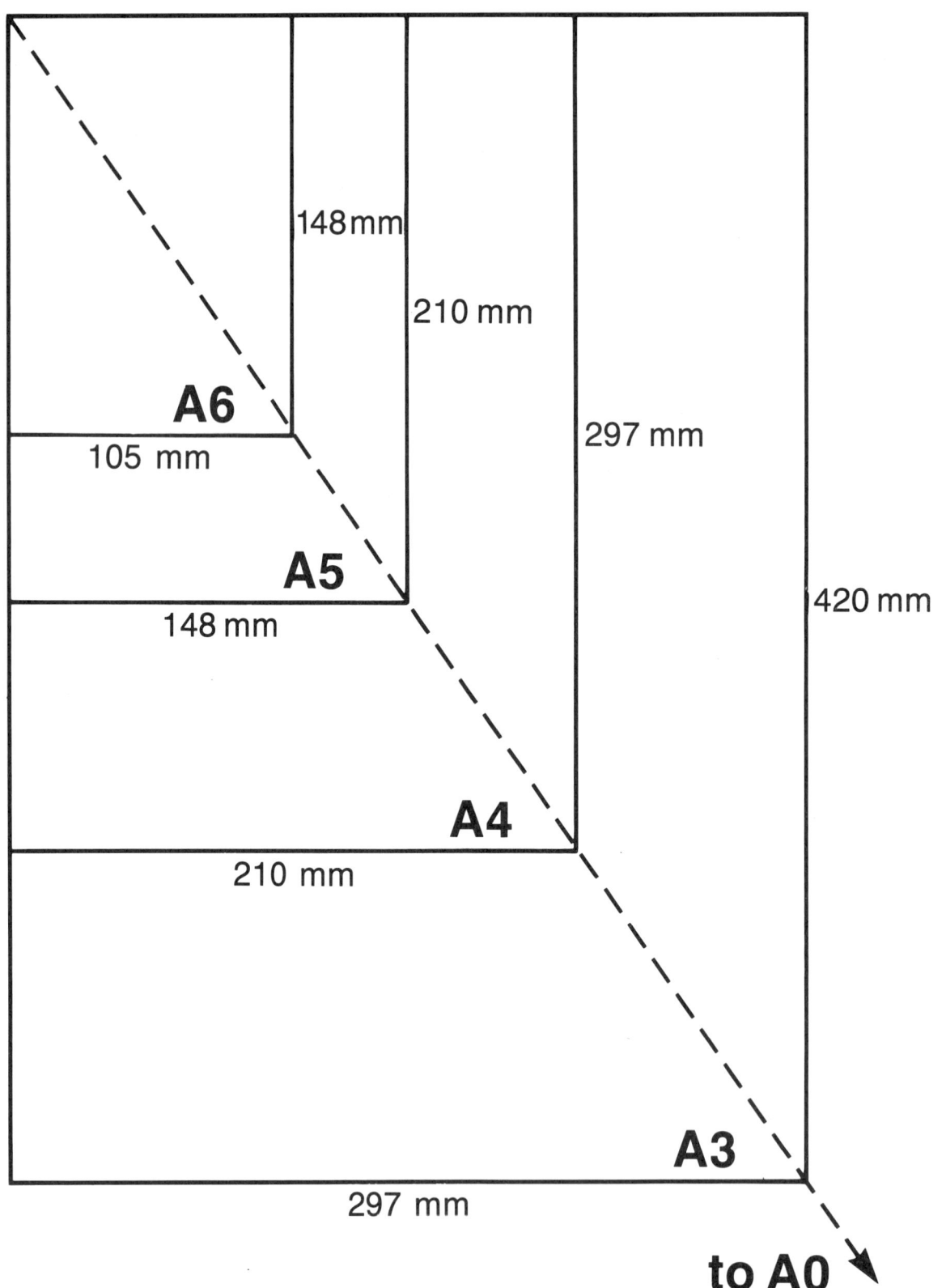

Standard Paper Sizes 2

Relationship of smaller sizes to the full A0 sheet

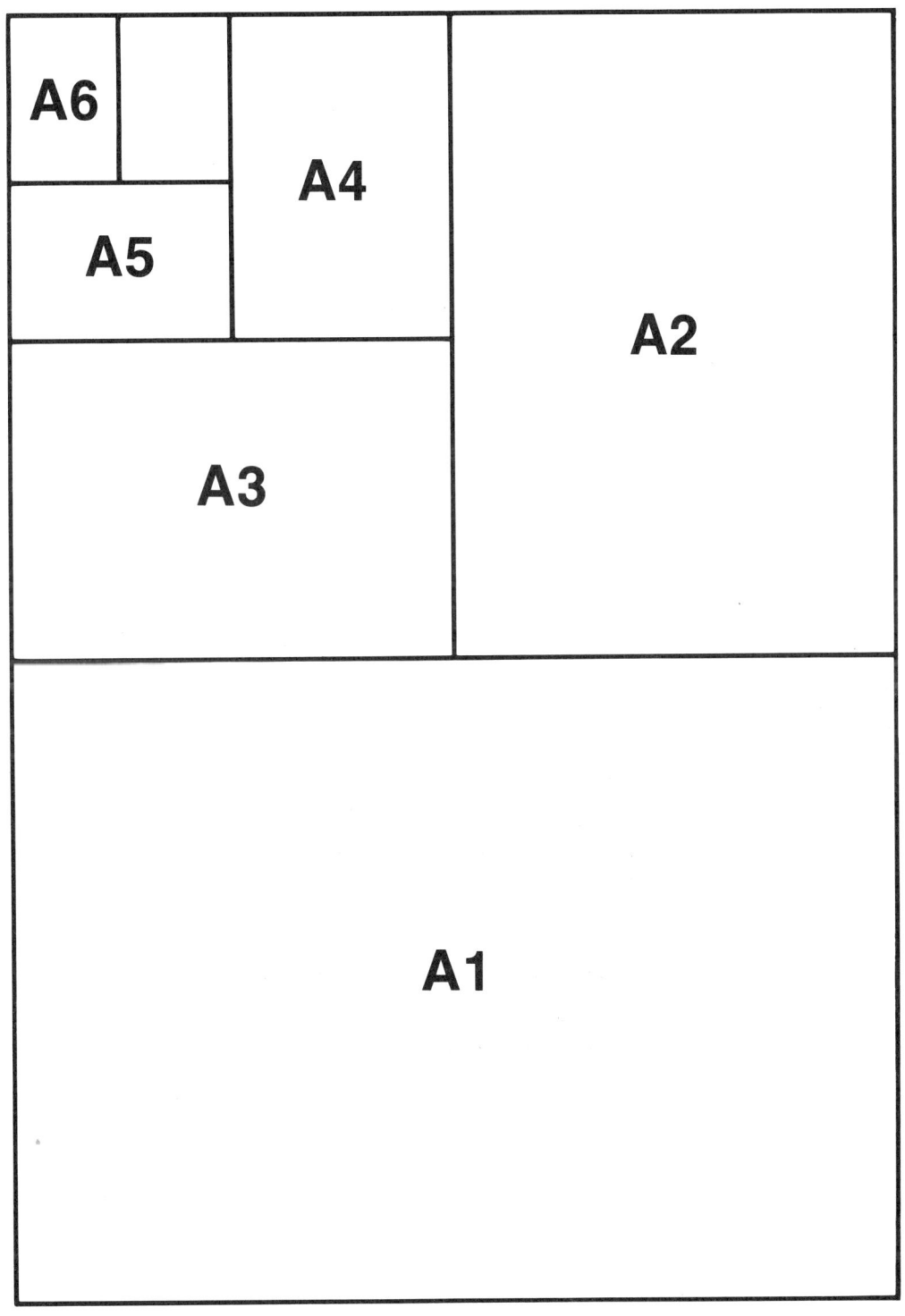

A0 sheet has area of 1m².
Edge dimensions in the ratio 1:√2

Widows and Orphans

This line of text has been
.... p
separated from the rest of the paragraph by an automatic page break. It is known as a WIDOW.

This paragraph is almost complete but unfortunately an automatic page break has caused an ORPHAN to
.... p
be left on the next page.

CHAPTER 6 | First steps in spreadsheet design and use

We have endeavoured in the early part of Chapter 6 in the student text to give a little background on the kind of problems which led to the development of spreadsheet software. You may feel that this introduction stands on its own, without additional teaching support. However, if you wish to run an introductory group session, then the first transparency master in Sequence 6.1 may be of use. The remainder of this sequence illustrates the basic terminology required for working with spreadsheets.

Perhaps the largest conceptual difficulty we have encountered when teaching the use of spreadsheet software to beginners, is that the computer system is there to do the calculations for us; our job is to describe to the computer exactly what calculations we want it to do.

For example, if we have a spreadsheet with a column of headings as in the diagram below, you will not have to wait long before a student tries to enter sample data in A3 and B3, painstakingly to calculate the product and to enter the *result* in C3. Of course, what we actually want entered in C3 is the instruction to multiply the contents of A3 by the contents of B3.

Another common problem is that students will enter numbers as text. A frequent reason for this is that until they know something about formatting, they find they cannot make a numerical entry appear as they wish. For example, they may wish to enter £10.00, not realising that their software almost certainly has a currency format; or they may not be happy with an input of 10.00 being displayed in a standard default format simply as 10. But for whatever reason, it is a common beginner's mistake.

The point being missed, is that the system can only perform arithmetic on numbers, not on groups of characters which happen to be figures, but which could equally well be alphabetic characters.

	A	B	C	D
1	QUANTITY	UNIT	TOTAL	
2		PRICE	VALUE	
3				
4				
5				
6				
7				

So what are the fundamental points to establish at the outset? We suggest:

1. That the system does the calculations – we tell it what calculations to do.
2. That any cell contents on which a calculation may be performed *must* be entered as numbers and not as a text string.
3. That when instructions concerning a calculation refer to a cell address, they mean that the arithmetic process described in the instruction is to be applied to the *value* present in the addressed cell.
4. That the *value* displayed in a cell is not necessarily the *content* of the cell. For example, with reference to the diagram above. If the content of A3 were 2 and the content of B3 were 6.50, we would (rightly) expect the cell C3 to display 13.00. But the *content* of the cell C3 would be of the form A3*B3.

These points could well be handled in a group teaching session before students tackle individual work. That is not to say that students will be away from the computers – far from it. But this is a time when it is probably most efficient for you as a tutor to have a rigid control over a common group activity, and if you decide to handle it this way, you may find Transparency 6.2 is a useful teaching aid.

Here is a suggested approach for this activity:

1. Enter text headings as in the diagram above.
   (*Learning*: how to enter text; entry on arrow keys (if the facility exists with your software); to combine entry with cursor movement to change the active cell to the one next required for an entry.)
   Note: No formatting – centring or right justification of text – at this stage.
2. Enter single figure values in A3 and B3.
   (*Learning*: distinguishing between text and numerical entry.)
3. Enter in C3 an appropriate 'formula' or instruction which you would give to suit the syntax requirements of your software.
   (*Learning*: the fundamentals of formula entry.)
4. Note the 'answer' appearing in cell C3, and with the cursor highlighting that cell, point out the status entry (usually at either top or bottom left side of screen) which gives the address of the active cell and its *content*, as distinct from the resultant display.
   (*Learning*: the difference between cell content and display.)
5. Move the cursor to A3 and enter a different quantity value.
   (*Learning*: *a* the contents of a cell may be changed by overwriting – no mention of protection or locking of cells at this stage. *b* recalculation is automatic and the new answer appears in C3, but, of course, the cell content of C3 is unchanged.)
6. Make yet another entry in A3, but this time as text – e.g. use ALPHA in Multiplan, initial inverted commas in SuperCalc, or whatever your software requires – and note the resulting ERROR message.
   (*Learning*: introduction to ERROR messages and reinforcement of concept that arithmetic must be performed on numbers, not strings of numeric characters.)

You could well extend this work further. For example:

7 Replace QUANTITY with QTY and make column A narrower – say, 4 characters wide.
(*Learning*: the setting of column width.)
8 Format cells B3 and C3 as Fixed, 2 decimal places; perhaps reformat as Currency.
(*Learning*: introduction to formatting.)
9 Depending on the facilities available, move column titles to sit squarely over the figures they describe.
(*Learning*: positioning of text.)

To reinforce the processes practised above, we suggest this group exercise. The plan is to produce a spreadsheet along the lines of the diagram below. Start in the 'home' cell, i.e. A1, or R1C1 in Multiplan. Set column A (or 1) to a width of 25, column B (or 2) to a width of 4. Appropriate formulae should be entered in D3, E3, F3. The range C3:F3 should be formatted as Fixed, 2 decimal places. Titles in the range C1:F2 should be right justified.

	A	B	C	D	E	F
1	DESCRIPTION	QTY	UNIT	TOTAL	VAT	AMOUNT
2			PRICE	VALUE		PAYABLE
3				0.00	0.00	0.00
4						

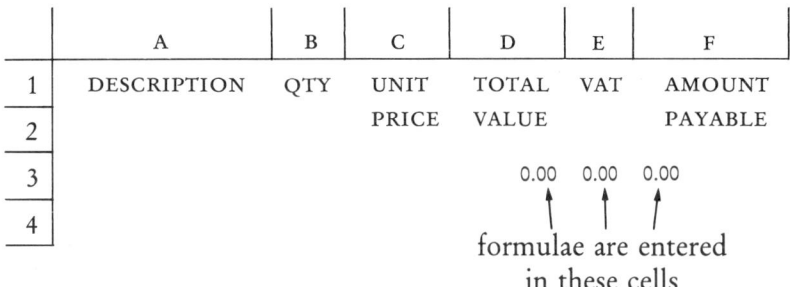

formulae are entered in these cells

There is no work here that has not been covered above, and hopefully all members of the group will contribute in producing a concensus view on how they should tackle the project successfully.

The correct operation of individual spreadsheets should be checked by insertion of appropriate data. You can throw in another small point at this stage: if a unit price is, say, £10.00, then the user need input only 10. The format will add the trailing zeros.

By this time, the students should be able to work through the first part of Chapter 6 on their own, but in the course of the Stock Value assignment, they are going to need to save their spreadsheet to disk. In fact, we wish to save the spreadsheet developed in the group work just completed for later extension, so this is a good opportunity to take the group through the saving and close down routine.

At the end of this chapter, we have provided a *pro forma* for you to complete and photocopy for distribution to your students, if you so wish. Its purpose is to act as an *aide-mémoire* for them when working on their own, and as you will see, it covers procedures like saving.

When ready for another group teaching session, there are several ways you can proceed: if you are working with students who are not too happy with percentages and have trouble in producing a formula in E3 of the kind 0.15*D3, you may well wish to divert in this direction. Spreadsheets are invaluable in helping people to develop their understanding of the principles underlying a process.

But if VAT is not a problem, then we move on to consider the question of how to construct the spreadsheet to deal with entries in rows below row 3. Surely, we do not have to write a new formulae for cells D4, E4, F4, then D5, E5, F5, etc?

This is your opportunity to introduce copying or replication. We prefer the term *replication* as a description of the process which automatically adjusts cell addresses when formulae are copied down to further rows; *copy* can then be used for an exact copy (where addresses are not adjusted). But we are well aware that such a distinction is not always made by spreadsheet software originators. For example, Lotus 1-2-3 always assumes replication when asked to copy unless cell references are specifically modified by $ prefixes to indicate an absolute address, which is copied unchanged.

Depending on the software you are using, you may find yourself getting involved in a discussion of *relative* vs. *absolute* addressing at this stage. You certainly will if you are using Multiplan and have used absolute addresses for the formulae R3C4:R3C6. To avoid this complication with Multiplan, we suggest that you teach the use of the arrow keys to move the cursor to indicate addresses used in formulae. This in fact produces relative addressing (e.g. in cell R3C5 we might have RC(−1)*0.15 meaning, '0.15 times the contents of the cell which is in the same row, but back one column'. If you do this, there is no need to refer to the terms absolute and relative addressing at this stage. We think it is best saved until a little later.

With any software, we can look on replication as the copying of a 'pattern' of interaction, which has been set up in one group of cells in the spreadsheet, so that the same effect is produced elsewhere on the sheet.

At this point, you can reinforce the principle of *range definition* – the demarcation top left and bottom right corners of the range – by getting the group to format in one operation the range of cells from C4 to F20 (or however far down you got your students to copy the formulae).

Using either copying (replication) or formatting of a group of cells, you are going to have to introduce the term *range* and Transparency sequence 6.3 offers illustrations of what does and does not constitute a valid range.

The spreadsheet, as it now stands, could be used for data entry – the weight you give to this activity will clearly depend on the nature of the student group. The sheet has still further potential for introducing new work, so it should be saved again, thus providing another opportunity to take the group through the saving and close down routine used by your software. It will be slightly different this time, of course, because the software will seek your assurance that you wish to overwrite the previous version of the file.

As we have indicated, more assignments can be built on this spreadsheet, and we offer the following ideas for development:

1 Columns D, E and F could be totalled using a SUM(range) function which is available in roughly that form in almost all spreadsheet software.

(*Learning*: the use of perhaps the most fundamental of a range of functions available within the software.)

2 Insert three rows before row 1.
(*Learning*: use of insert command, but much more importantly, to see what has happened to formulae which have been moved to later row numbers as a result of this insertion.)

3 A title could now be entered in, say, B2, which will extend beyond the width of the cell.
(*Learning*: the opportunity for the group to investigate what happens in these circumstances. It will depend on the software you are using; some allows overflow to the right into any unoccupied cells, whilst Multiplan, for example, requires the user deliberately to break down the partition between cells in order to achieve this.)

Depending on the ability level of your group, you might like to pose the problem of the Chancellor changing the VAT rate. The formulae built into column E assume 15%; would it not be better if column E were headed in E1 'VAT @' and a value entered in E2, which would be formatted to display the value as a percentage? Thus if, for example, 0.15 were entered in E2, the column heading would appear as:

VAT @

15%

Then the formulae in column E would not make specific reference to the factor 0.15, but rather to the contents of cell E2.

So the formula in E3 would be D3*E2. But if we were to replicate this formula, we would have a nonsense in subsequent rows because E2 would be changed to E3, E4, E5, etc., in successive rows. What we want is replication so far as the reference to cells in column D is concerned, but an unchanging *absolute* address reference to E2.

We believe this is quite a good way of introducing the distinction between relative and absolute addressing in a group situation: first let students develop the concept of 'pattern' relationships and appreciate their importance in replication; and only then introduce something which forces the need for absolute addressing.

By this time, you have covered in group work most of the key features which students will use in assignments described in Chapter 6. The use of *windows* – or the superior titles facility available in some spreadsheet software – which prevent titles scrolling off screen, as more entries are added to the spreadsheet, could be introduced in group work. But in our view it is better handled with individuals as and when the need arises. The same is true of printed output, although this is a topic where the principles of setting the range, margins and page length could reasonably be covered in group work, if you wish.

For some groups, there are some interesting spin-off exercises that you may wish to pursue. For example, although we may choose to display a number to one or two decimal places, it is held much more accurately in the computer; the display is correctly rounded up or down as appropriate. In extreme cases, this can lead to some silly display errors. Consider the example given overleaf.

Decimal point format	A	B	C	D	
	n	n/1.6	n/1.7	sum(A:C)	
3 dp	1	0.625	0.588	2.213	both of which are acceptable. However...
1 dp	1.0	0.6	0.6	2.2	
2 dp	1.00	0.63	0.59	2.21	here is a problem, because it is clear that $1 + 0.63 + 0.59 = 2.22...$
0 dp	1	1	1	2	and $1 + 1 + 1 = 2$ is clearly a nonsense.

People tend to lose faith in spreadsheets which do not appear to add up. You certainly would not introduce this problem to the mathematically weak. But it makes sense to cover it with students who can take it, and such students could be introduced to one or two other functions as well, such as INT(eger) and MOD(ulus). A simple spreadsheet, which involves these functions in a practical situation, enables the time an individual spends on it to be recorded against the specific activities. The automatic totalling of times, entered in hours and minutes, is necessarily going to involve INT and MOD functions.

If you have a very able group, you might wish to introduce the conditional function IF . . . (THEN, ELSE), but in our view, this is moving slightly further than is intended with this introductory text. There are, however, three functions which you could introduce to almost any group: MAX, MIN and AVERAGE. A very simple spreadsheet using these functions could comprise a list of people in your group with their heights. If you wanted to make more out of this example, you could use the sheet to calculate deviations from the mean, or convert heights from metres and centimetres to feet and inches.

The scope is endless! You will probably have many ideas that you will want to introduce with your own student groups. All we have tried to do is to give you a few 'starter' ideas, which are additional to those provided in the student text, so that you can, if you wish, develop a tutor-centred approach to complement the student-centred approach of the student text. The single transparency, 6.4, may serve as a jumping-off point for further work.

First steps in spreadsheet design and use

Your spreadsheet software is called: _____

	Lotus 1–2–3	Multiplan	SuperCalc
Command file containing your spreadsheet software is:	123.COM	MP.COM	SC.COM
When the spreadsheet software is loaded, available commands may not be visible. To activate commands press:	Forward slash (/)	Commands *are* visible on loading	Forward slash (/)
To select commands, press the initial letter of the command word:	True	True	True
To enter a string:	Precede entry with '(apostrophe) unless 1st char is alphabetic	A for Alpha	Precede entry with " (inverted commas)
To enter a formula:	+ (or – if appropriate)	=	No special symbol needed
To enter numbers there is no need to begin with a special character:	True	True	True
Cursor movement is by use of 'arrow' keys:	True	True	True
To go to a remote address:	F5, enter address	G (Goto command), R & address	=, enter address
To change column width:	/W C F and required col. width	F W and required col. width	/F C and required col. width
To format numerical entries:	/R F, select format and range	F C, specify range, TAB twice, SPACE to code. If necessary TAB again to set decimal places	/F

To delete entries in a range of cells:	/R E plus address(es)	B plus address(es)	/B plus address(es)
To abandon spreadsheet:	/W E Y	T C Y	/Z Y
To save a spreadsheet:	/F S plus file name	T S plus file name	/S plus file name
To load a spreadsheet from disk:	/F R plus file name	T L plus file name	/L plus file name
	Can use arrow keys to select file name	Use arrow keys to show directory of current disk drive and select file	
To replicate formulae:	/C then specify range from which to copy and range to copy to	C then choose from (R)ight, (D)own or (F)rom, then specify range from which to copy and range to copy to	/R then specify range from which to copy and range to copy to

First steps in spreadsheet design and use

Your spreadsheet software is called: _____

Command file
containing your
spreadsheet software is:

When the spreadsheet
software is loaded,
available commands
may not be visible. To
activate commands
press:

To select commands,
press the initial letter of
the command word:

To enter a string:

To enter a formula:

To enter numbers there
is no need to begin with
a special character:

Cursor movement is by
use of 'arrow' keys:

To go to a remote
address:

To change column
width:

To format numerical
entries:

To delete entries in a
range of cells:

To abandon
spreadsheet:

To save a spreadsheet:

To load a spreadsheet
from disk:

To replicate formulae:

Chapter 6 – Transparency sequence 1
Introduction to spreadsheet concepts

Transparency reference

6.1.1 An illustration of a simple analysis sheet. By overlaying a blank transparency one may build up a full example, which could subsequently be transferred to a spreadsheet.

6.1.2 This defines the terms *row*, *column*, *cell* and facilitates initial discussion on the kind of entries which are possible.

6.1.3 An illustration of cell addressing techniques for two styles of spreadsheets; one with columns identified by letters and rows by numbers, the other in the style of Multiplan with both rows and columns identified by numbers.

Chapter 6 – Transparency 6.2

In our experience, this very simple grid is one of the most effective teaching tools when dealing with introductory spreadsheet work. The cells need to be large, so the grid is restricted to four columns and four or five rows.

In use, overlay the grid with a blank transparency, so that the original grid can be used repeatedly. Then take one colour for the actual cell entry and a second colour for what is displayed at that cell position on screen.

Chapter 6 – Transparency sequence 3
Illustrations of valid and invalid ranges

To use this sequence you will need the grid shown in Transparency 6.2, because the following transparencies are designed to overlay it.

Notes

Transparency reference

6.3.1 A range is described in general terms (i.e. as extending from the top left-hand corner to the bottom right-hand corner.)

6.3.2 An example of an invalid range. It cannot be defined in terms of diagonally opposite references.

6.3.3 The first of three special cases; here the range is part of a single row.

6.3.4 The second special case: the range is part of a single column.

6.3.5 The third special case: a single cell is actually a range (indeed, Lotus 1–2–3 would refer to it in the range context as, for example, C3..C3).

Chapter 6 – Transparency 6.4
Spreadsheet applications

This transparency suggests categories of applications for which spreadsheet software is well suited.

What if applications are those where the user, having set up a mathematical model of his problem, substitutes alternative values for the parameters, over which s/he can exercise control. These are then used to check the sensitivity of the bottom line to variations in each parameter, or simply to determine the absolute effect of a particular change. Budgeting applications are obvious candidates for spreadsheet work; they can readily be extended to provide full cash flow information. What we call *framework* applications, some people call *template* applications; they are of the kind where, for a given application, a spreadsheet contains all essential text and all formulae in place, but no data. This sheet is then available to be loaded, used with current data and the completed sheet is then filed under another name (usually making reference to the date on which the data was current). The template or framework sheet is then still available to be called on a subsequent occasion for use with a new set of data.

Records processing applications are usually more suitable for database software than spreadsheets, but we have come across small businesses that keep such things as personnel records on spreadsheets.

There are, of course, many other spreadsheet application areas, but they are likely either to be beyond the scope of the software available (e.g. goal-seeking) or the mathematical understanding of the students (e.g. forecasting techniques involving linear or multiple regression).

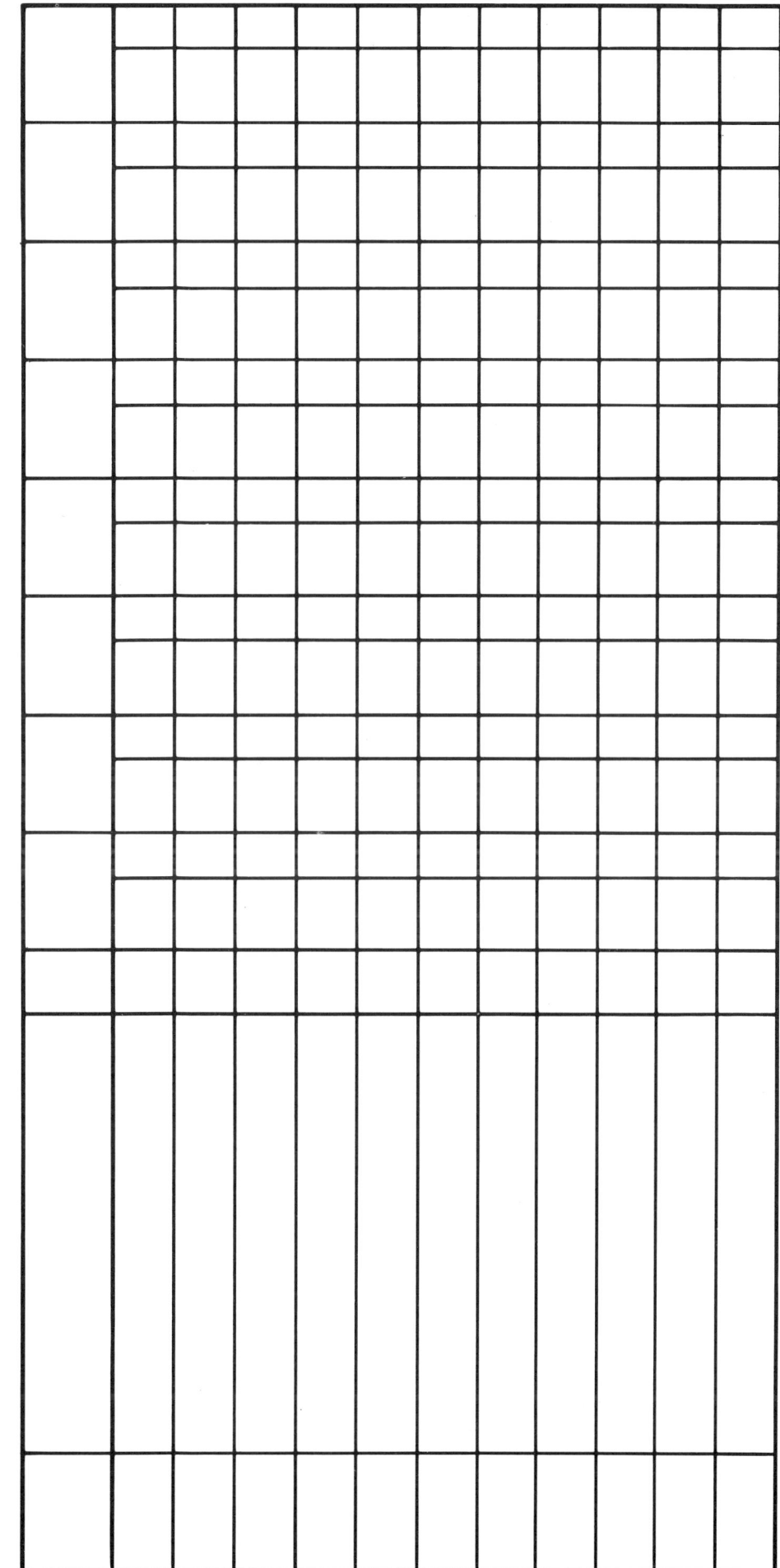

Spreadsheets

Spreadsheets facilitate an ordered approach to the arithmetic processing of columns or rows of figures.

Entries are made into **cells**
- defined as the intersection of **rows** and **columns**

	column
row	cell

Entries may be . . .
- **text (strings)**
- **numbers**
- **formulae** (electronic spreadsheets only)

Cell Addresses

Cells are identified by addresses which relate to the relevant row and column identities.

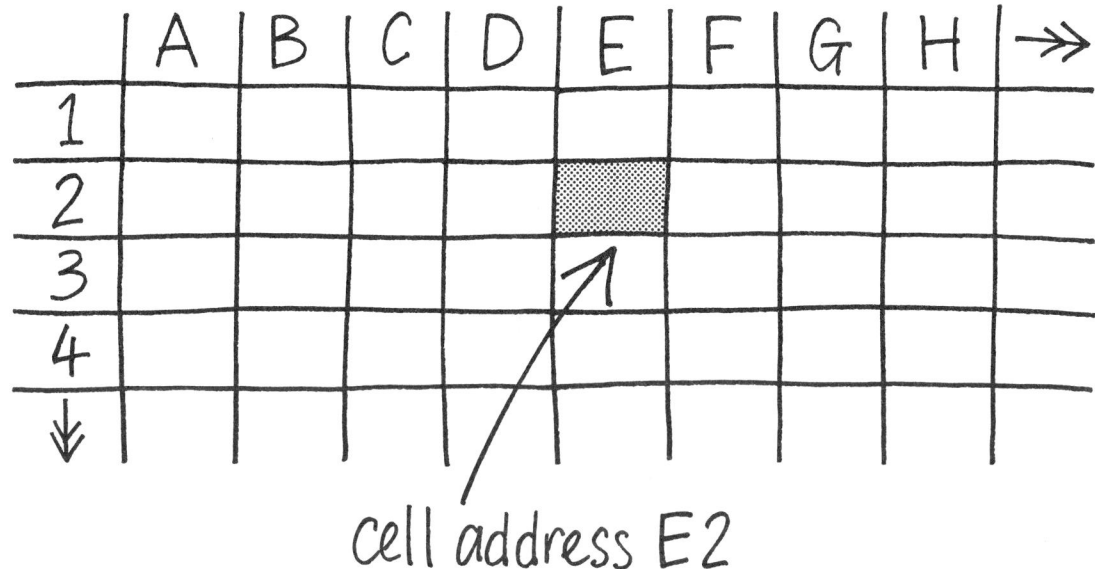

cell address E2

cell address R2C5

6.2

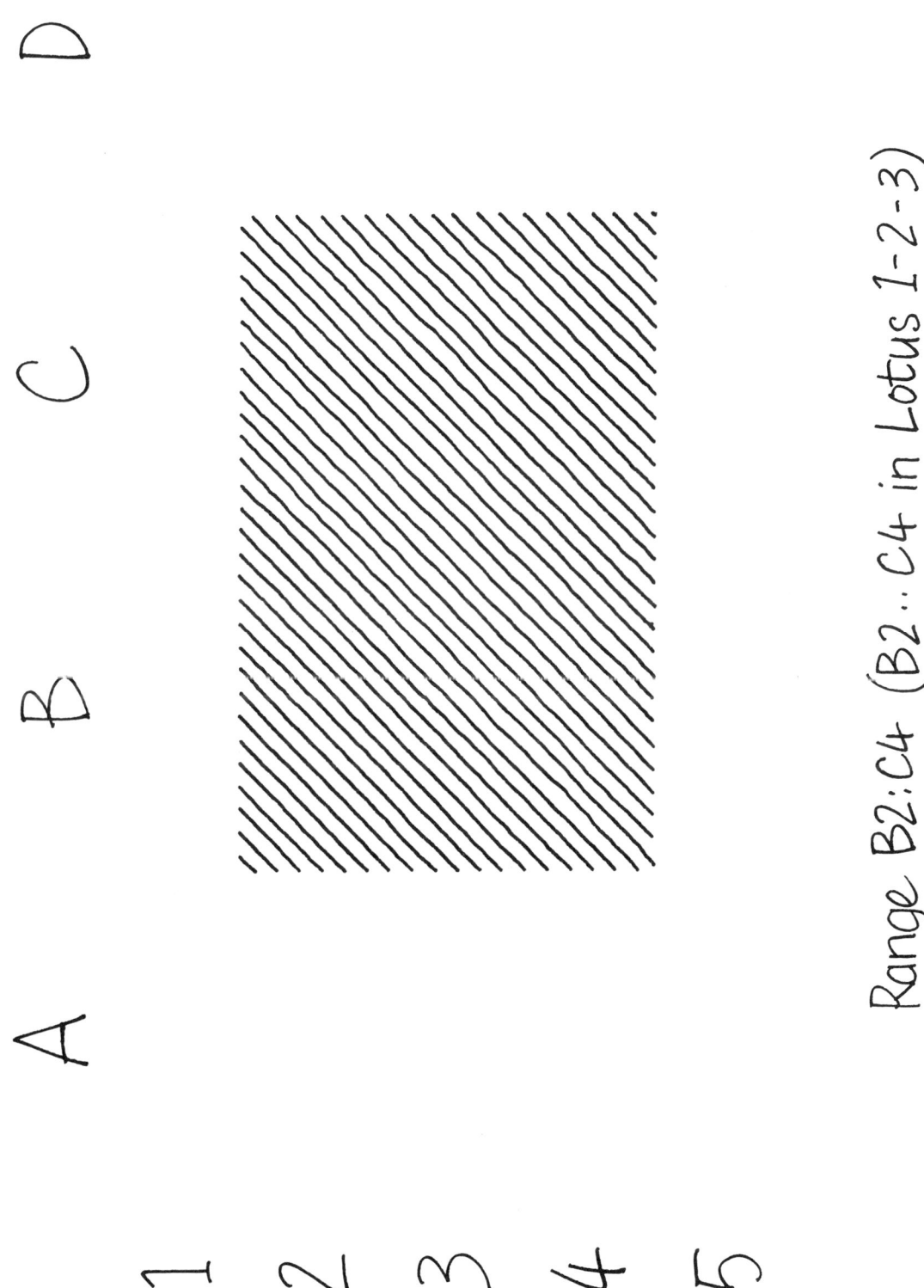

Range B2:C4 (B2..C4 in Lotus 1-2-3)

6.3.2

Not a valid range - must be a rectangle

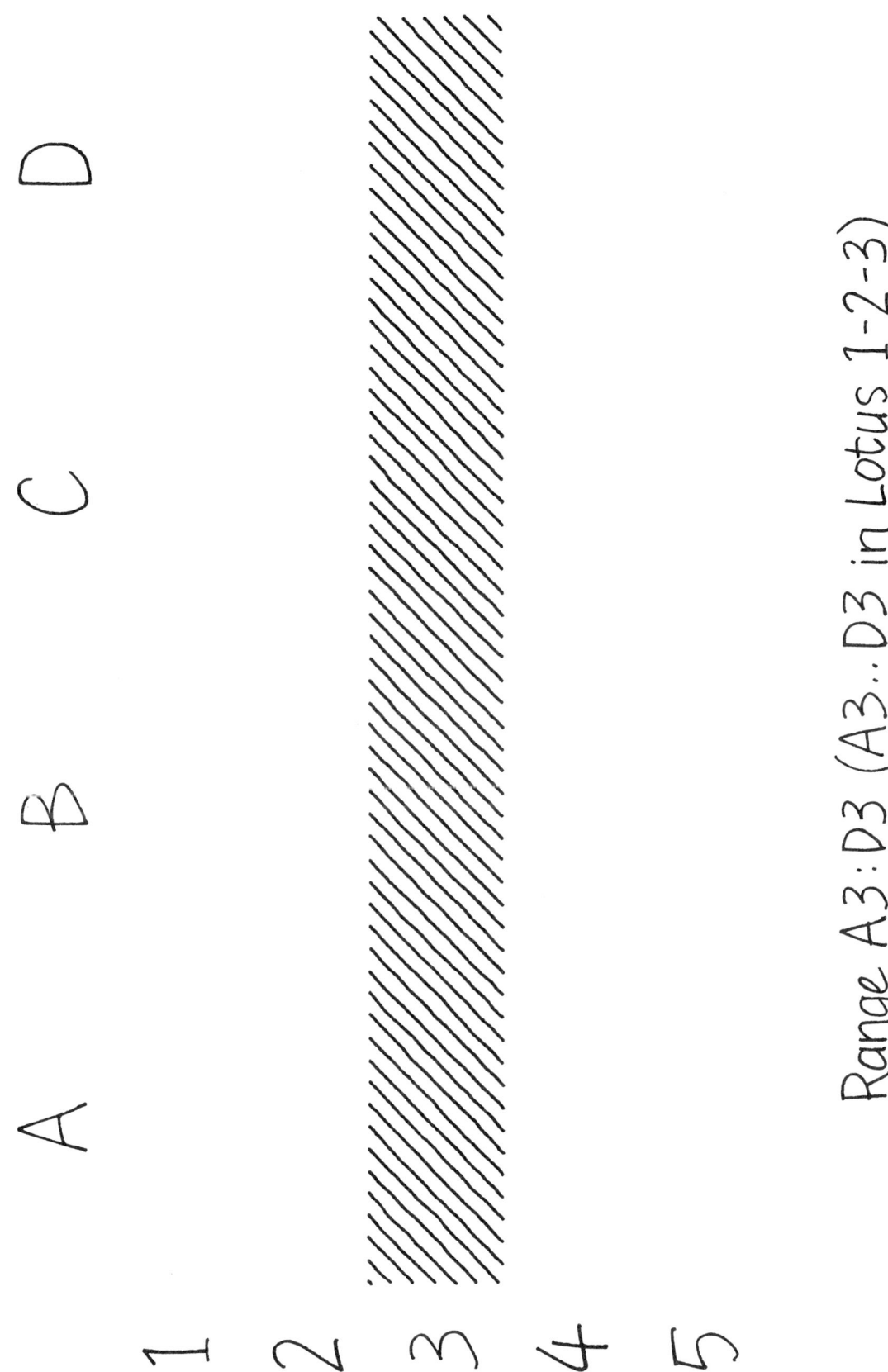

Range A3:D3 (A3..D3 in Lotus 1-2-3)

6.3.4

Range B2:B4 (B2..B4 in Lotus 1-2-3)

A single cell is the smallest possible range (in this example, C3)

Spreadsheet Applications

A spreadsheet is ideal for applications which

- involve some repeated data amendment or processing of some kind
- are not so complex as to warrant the design and construction of dedicated software
- can be handled effectively by end-users, e.g.

  - *What if* applications
  - Budgeting applications
  - 'Framework' applications
  - Simple records processing applications

CHAPTER 7 | Communications on computer systems

In Chapter 7 of the student text we cover the background of early attempts at communication with centralized computing facilities, which led to processing power and data being brought nearer to users, as technological developments allowed this to be done.

This soon leads to an illustration of wide area networks (WAN) with minicomputers and mainframes being linked to each other (see Transparency sequence 7.1). We say nothing in the text about the considerations necessary in the setting up of computer links over wide area networks, because it is not essential for an appreciation of the concept of computer networking.

However, as an example of a typical approach to a systems problem, the analysis into seven 'layers' and systematic approach for agreeing the standards for each layer from the bottom up, might be useful for some student groups. In Transparency 7.2 we provide a display of the 7-stage Open Systems Interconnection (OSI) model, and the associated notes provide a parallel illustration in terms of a long-distance telephone call; relating technical jargon to everyday experience.

The student text also spends some time on local area networks (LAN), and diagrams used in the text are reproduced as transparency masters (together with some other diagrams) in Sequences 7.3 and 7.4. Sequence 7.3 provides a smooth transition from wide to local area networks, and covers network topologies with especial reference to questions of system resilience in the face of hardware failure. In Sequence 7.4 we look at the contention problem and the way leading network products either cope with it or avoid it.

We have tended to dwell on local area networks, to the exclusion of multi-user systems, simply because the tendency has been to meet the need for intercommunicating micro-computers, with shared resources in a building or on a simple site, by using LAN technology. Operating systems which will run multi-user microcomputer systems have not yet really caught on with user organizations. There are several reasons for this which need not concern us particularly; but the point which must be stressed, is that this situation is likely to change rapidly in the course of the next year or two.

Multi-user software, both at operating system level and at applications program level is necessarily much more complex than the equivalents for single user systems. Essentially, the problem is to let each user feel that the system is entirely theirs, whilst ensuring that their activities in no way interfere with or invalidate the activities of another user (who also thinks that the whole system is theirs). Multi-user systems are ideal for sharing the use of software or data; a network may well be better for sharing expensive physical resources. Multi-user systems will cater for no more than 32 users in realistic terms; networks may handle substantially more, but of course the response time is worsened as the network traffic increases.

We believe this is one of the most rapidly changing areas covered by the student text, and if you are going to support student work with additional material, you would be advised to read and use weekly and monthly trade technical publications for up-to-the-minute information.

Another example of rapid change in the field of data communication which we do not discuss in the student text is facsimile transmission, because although it uses bit image techniques, it is not, at present, associated directly with the use of computers. Instead, we dwell on text transmission, using electronic mail. Yet what is the trend now? More and more businesses are taking on fax; it is growing far more rapidly than e-mail.

Why is this? We think there are two reasons: one is operational simplicity; the other relates to the problem we mention in the student text of e-mail communication being restricted to those who use the same e-mail system, whereas fax communication is available between any two fax machines in any place.

The real virtue of fax is, of course, its ability to transmit non-textual information – graphics, signatures, etc. But many firms use it for the transmission of straightforward typed text. The scanning of an image for fax transmission is similar in principle to the scanning of documents for direct input to a computer system, usually as part of a desk-top publishing application.

Certainly a simple character set, such as we have in the western world, could be transmitted more economically using bit patterns to represent individual characters than creating a bit image of the characters. But not so in Japan, where the written language contains literally thousands of characters; it is small wonder that the innovations which have led to modern Group 3 fax have originated largely in the Far East.

Although, as we have said, fax communication is currently independent of computer systems, you should be aware that several companies are developing pc/fax communications, in which the bit image data received is input directly into a micro-computer and stored ready for subsequent manipulation.

Chapter 7 – Transparency sequence 1
The need for networking and an introduction to wide area networks

Notes

Transparency reference   7.1.1   This transparency shows schematically the kind of centralized computer systems which were common up to the mid 1980s. The limitations worth emphasizing are:

1 The system has very little resilience – if the central computer goes down, then the whole system is off the air.
2 The shared lines from the concentrators to the mainframe can readily become overloaded and hence cause unacceptable delays for terminal users.

In its day, it was an adequate solution to the problem of many users accessing and interacting with shared data. But now technological advances allow us to bring both data and computing power closer to the end users.

7.1.2 Here is a schematic representation of a distributed system, which achieves the same ends as the system shown in 7.1.1. But now:

1 Resilience is much better. If the mainframe goes down, only the data held centrally becomes unavailable. If a minicomputer fails, only those terminals connected directly to it are out of commission.
2 The data most needed is close to the terminals which are likely to use it.

7.1.3 This transparency illustrates the need for handling WANs in an organized way.

Diagram *a* is a representation of the simple connection of two computers. This could, in theory, be an exclusive direct link. But it is not long before one of the parties to the connection wishes also to communicate with a third computer, which is already linked to a fourth. Very quickly, a 'cat's cradle' situation develops – see diagram *b*.

The obvious solution is for each computer to link to a central switching facility or flexibility point. The star configuration of diagram *c* illustrates this.

As the area under consideration grows larger, so we see the network expand into a cluster topology as shown in diagram *d*.

Chapter 7 – Transparency 7.2
The Open Systems Interconnection (OSI) model

The Open Systems Interconnection (OSI) model breaks down the overall problem of data communication into seven protocol levels. In this transparency we look at each level in turn and relate the function of each protocol to the more familiar situation of making a telephone call.

Let us set the scene. Your friend has recently taken some important examinations and is now on holiday at the Hotel San Marco in Venice, having asked you to telephone the results through the moment they are published.

Level 1 *Physical control.* A pair of channels which can transmit the human voice must be provided if our telephone call can go ahead. The process is to convert the human sound waves into analogue electrical waves, so that they can be transmitted down the telephone lines. The electrical waves are converted back to sound waves by the telephone receiver at the far end.

With computer output (in the form of a stream of bits at one of two voltage levels representing 0 or 1) the conversion to electrical waves and the reconversion to bits at the far end is usually performed by a *modem*.

Level 2 *Data link*. In a telephone conversation – even a local one, let alone one to Italy – there will be occasions when the sounds received are unclear. Because we know the context of what is being said, we can quite often compensate for these 'errors' (they are errors because they do not faithfully replicate the transmitted signal). But sometimes the message may be so indistinct that your friend asks for a retransmission by saying: 'Sorry, I didn't get that. Could you say it again?'

The electronic transmission of data has the same parallel. The transmitted data is contained within a 'frame', the main purpose of which is to detect and correct, through a very complex check digit system (involving 16 bits) any errors in the data stream.

Level 3 *Network control*. So far we have established the availability of a two-way communication path with built-in error control. But we have not yet established a connection with Venice. The public switched telephone network (PSTN) provides a system, which allows one user to address any other user; it involves a dialling tone, the generation of pulses which set up the route, ringing tone and of course, it rings the bell of the addressed user to attract attention. How the call is routed, whether by land line or satellite, microwave links or any combination of these, is of no significance to the user.

With electronic transmission of data there are some 14 different types of 'packet'; the detail need not concern us, but it may be of interest to note that they fall into three main categories.
1 Those used solely for the transport of data (data packets).
2 Those used solely for control purposes (between terminal and exchange).
3 Those used for setting up and clearing down calls (these may, but need not contain user data).

The first three levels are those incorporated in British Telecom's X25 packet switching protocol, and they could equally be fulfilled by other protocols. They are the concern of the provider of the network. From Level 4 onwards the protocols are 'end to end', i.e., they concern the end user, not the network provider.

Level 4 *Transport*. The telephone analogy here, is that when the path has been set up and the phone at the far end has been picked up, the person answering follows a well-established routine, saying, 'Hotel San Marco'. Your response is to ask to be put through to your friend. At the end of your conversation there is another exchange of an expected form of words, such as, 'Bye now', 'See you soon'. Without conventions such as these, chaos would result.

With data communications, conventions are not yet quite so uniformly understood, because at the outset each major computer manufacturer went their own way. The International Standards Organization is attempting to deal with this problem and Level 4 is of key importance in this. It is the level where, if agreed standards are adhered to, the communication process is made independent of both the network and the application.

Level 5 *Session control.* In the telephone analogy, we have now reached the point of conversation. Intuitively, we know who is going to speak next and who is ready to listen. What stops both participants talking at once, or conversely, both lapsing into silence, waiting for each other to say something? We tend to prompt each other with questions, confirm that we have understood a point by saying, 'mm', 'yes' and so on.

But with data communication there is no room for intuition, and protocols for establishing the smooth flow of 'conversation' from end to end have to be established.

Level 6 *Control of presentation.* It was just as well when we started our call to Venice that the operator at the Hotel San Marco understood English. This is the essential point of protocols at Level 6. Either the two terminals must share a common language, or they must incorporate translators into a third common language.

Level 7 *The user's application.* In our telephone conversation analogy, the whole object of the exercise was to tell our friend about the examination results. That is the application in this case.

In the data communication case, it could be the transfer of accounting data files from a subsidiary to its parent company. Whatever the application, its success depends on agreed standards being followed at all levels in the model we have considered.

Chapter 7 – Transparency sequence 3
Drawing the line between wide and local area networks; network topology

Notes

Transparency reference

7.3.1 It may be as well to remind students of exactly what needs to be transmitted to enable data to be sent from one computer to another. It is a series of electrical pulses (nominally 5v or 0v) as illustrated here in which shows the byte pattern for the letter T.

With WANs, the data transmission is to a remote computer located off-site and so it must use the public switched telephone network (PSTN). The bit stream of pulses cannot be handled in its original form; the information the bytes contain is coded onto a different type of electrical signal (a *carrier*) which the PSTN can handle, and the original bit pattern extracted (demodulated) at the far end. Transmission rates are fairly slow, from a few hundred Bauds (bits per second) to a few thousand Bauds.

With LANs, the wiring is local, within a site, perhaps within a building. No modulation is required, because the pulses are sent through dedicated cables, not circuits designed for telephony.

7.3.2 When electrical pulses are sent down a transmission line they gradually deteriorate as shown in this transparency. In some systems (e.g. with a bus topology – see 7.3.3) this deterioration effectively determines the length of the network. In others (e.g. using a ring topology) the deteriorating pulse is used to trigger the generation of a new pulse, so that signal deterioration is not a limiting factor on the network length.

7.3.3 We have now made reference to the three major *network topologies*: *star* (or cluster) which was introduced in the context of WANs in 7.1; *bus* (or linear) and *ring*.

Occasionally, one will find a LAN using the star topology; in such cases the computers use existing telephone cabling to save the expense of introducing new cabling specifically for the network. But much more commonly either bus or ring topology is used and the LANs described in 7.4 employ one or other of these.

This transparency can be used to discuss the resilience of each system in the event of equipment failure or a break in the transmission line.

1. With the *star* configuration, a failure of the computer at the hub could be serious, but if at least one of the peripheral machines offers the same facilities a straight substitution could get all stations bar one going again. Similarly, a cable break will only affect one station.
2. The situation is not quite so good with a *bus* system. Here a cable break could cut off a considerable number of workstations from, say, the file-server or a high quality printer which might be connected to the bus on the other side of the break. In regard to equipment failure, the key items would be the disk store and the computer acting as file-server. Some systems keep a second disk store on line with continuous back-up from one disk to the other, so that this cause of failure is eliminated. As in 1 above, quick recovery from failure of the file-server is possible by straight substitution of a similar machine carrying the same software, taken from elsewhere in the network.
3. It is argued that with a bus system, even though a cable break may prevent a number of stations from undertaking useful work, because they cannot get at the resources they need, there will be at least some, perhaps many, stations the 'right' side of the break, which can continue to work uninterrupted. This is not the case with a simple *ring* system. A break in that and everybody is off the air.

This problem has been tackled in various ways, but perhaps the simplest solution currently available, which balances the conflicting requirements of good reliability and reasonable cost, is that put forward by IBM. Their LAN is a ring which in physical layout looks almost like a star.

7.3.4 This is a representation of the IBM token ring network, the physical arrangement of which is referred to as a 'star wired logical ring'. It implies a hierarchical wiring arrangement in which individual work stations in a given work area are wired to a wiring cabinet, and then the cabinets associated with each work area are linked on a ring system.

The advantages of such a system are that:

1. Faults can be by-passed easily.
2. Diagnosis of faults is made easier due to the centralized points.
3. It is easy to add work stations (up to the cabinet capacity) or to move them within an area.

Chapter 7 – Transparency sequence 4
Local Area Networks

Notes

Transparency reference

7.4.1 and 7.4.2 appear on one page in this manual and will need photocopying individually before being made into transparencies.

7.4.1 In principle, the function of any LAN is to transmit packets of data from one address to another on the network. Such packets, often called datagrams, must include the addresses of destination and source, as well as the data itself. Other digits relate to checking procedures which ensure data integrity.

7.4.2 This defines the contention problem.

7.4.3 Ethernet type products always use a bus network arrangement. Since the essence of the Ethernet approach is to check to see that the line is clear before transmitting, one might expect to avoid collision problems. The only reason for collision arising is that electricity takes a finite time to travel down a transmission line. It follows that the greater the length of the bus, the greater is the chance of collision occurring.

7.4.4 The procedure followed by an Ethernet type LAN when a collision is detected, is given in detail.

7.4.5 This transparency points to two systems which avoid contention problems, instead of allowing them to happen and then dealing with the effect as does Ethernet.

The first of these, polling each station in turn, is a technique often used in process control operations. Although not fast, it is totally predictable – you know exactly when the next opportunity will occur for a given station to send data.

Token-passing principles can be applied to both bus and ring topologies, but the commercially important system is the token ring system.

7.4.6a–e appear on one page in this manual and will need photocopying individually before being made into transparencies.

7.4.6 This series of overlays illustrates the token ring principle.

7.4.6a The sending station, on the left, prepared data for transmission and waits for the free token to arrive.

7.4.6b The sender changes the free token to busy token and appends the data; token continues round the ring.

7.4.6c At other work-stations *en route* – not shown – the token is examined to see if either of the addresses it carries is theirs. Since it is not, the token is sent on round the ring, until it reaches the work-station with the destination address. The receiver then copies the data addressed to it.

7.4.6d The token with the copied data continues its way back to the sender, being inspected by intervening stations to check addresses.

7.4.6e The sending station, having confirmed that its address is the one in the 'sender's address' part of the datagram, removes its data and issues the free token. (*Note*: that it cannot monopolise the token because now the next or subsequent stations have the opportunity to seize and use it before it comes past the original sending station again in a free condition.)

Centralized Computer System

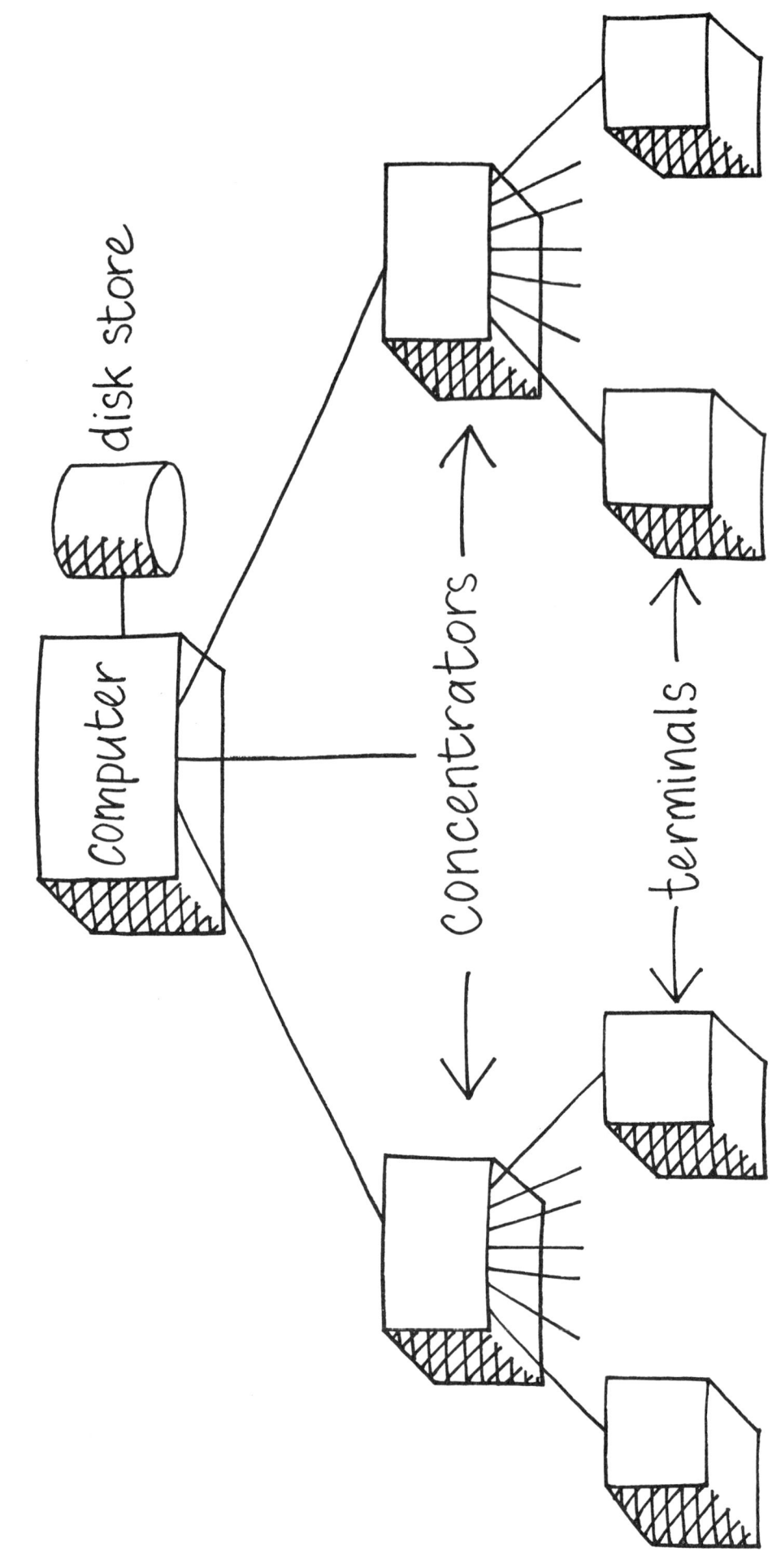

Distributed Computer System

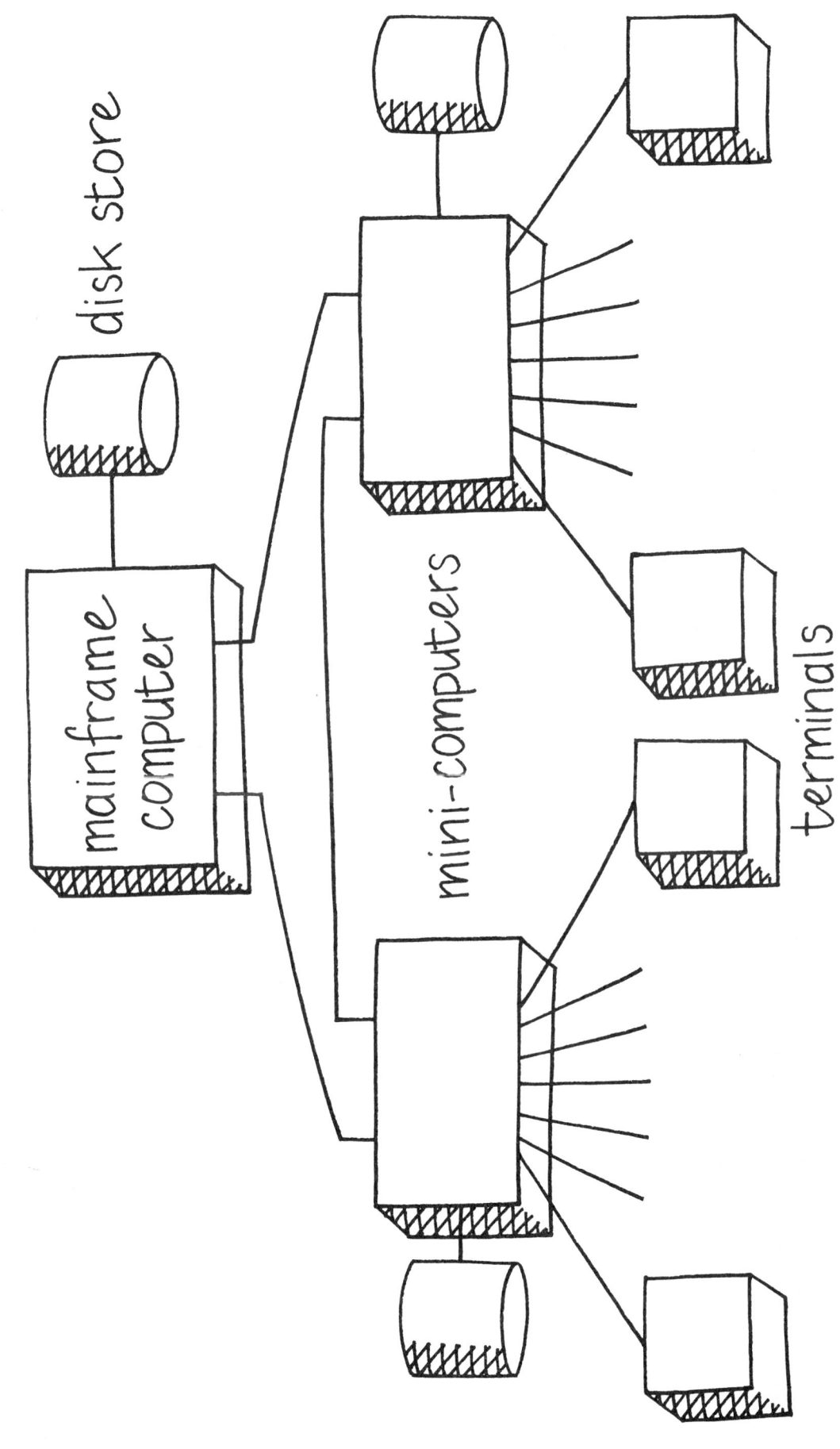

Development of Wide Area Networks

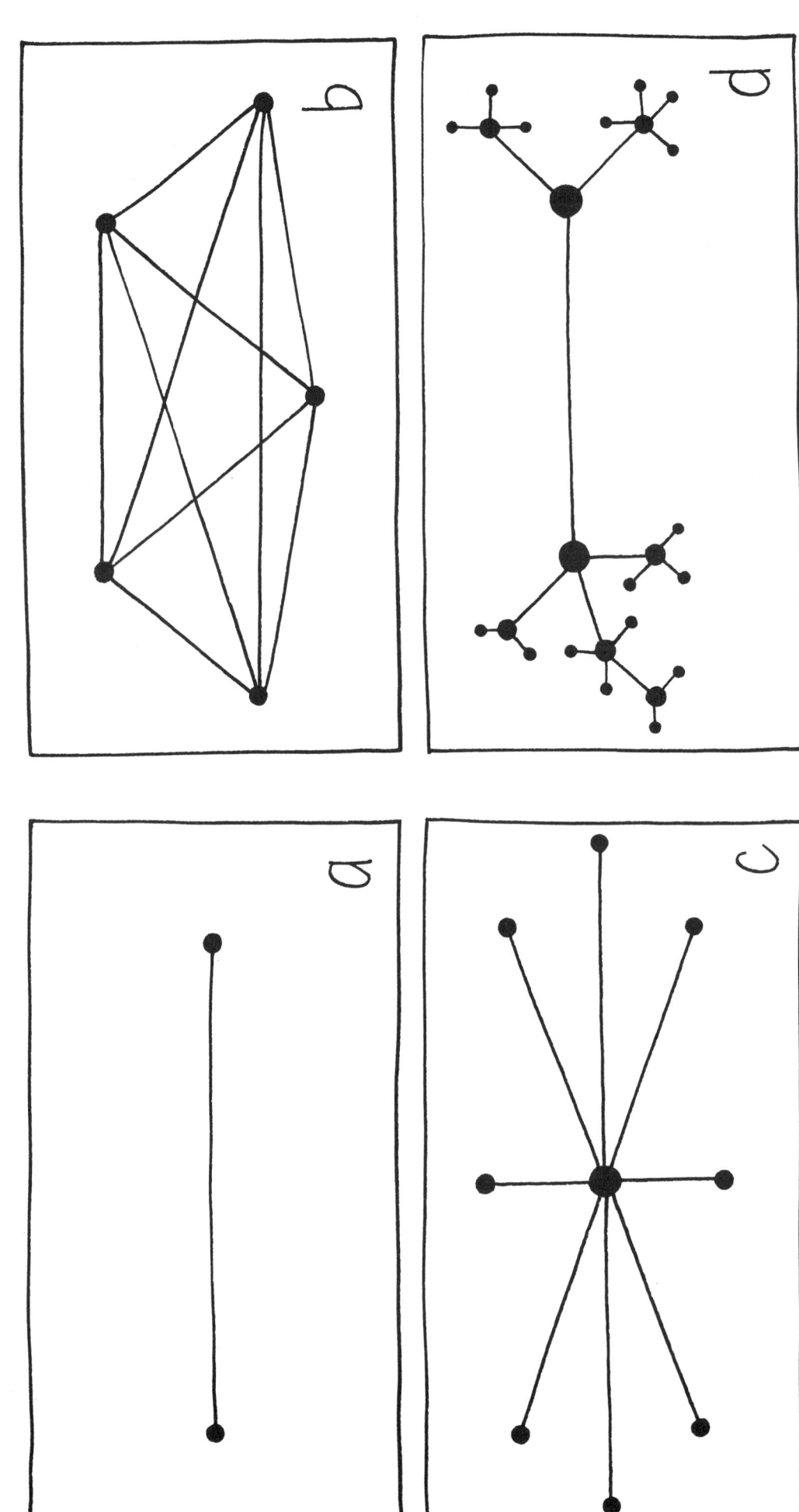

Standardization of Communications Protocols

Protocols – the rules and conventions for transmitting data.

The **ISO** (**I**nternational **S**tandards **O**rganization) has proposed a model for the definition of protocol standards – the **O**pen **S**ystems **I**nterconnection model (**OSI**). It defines seven protocol levels.

Layer	Function
7 Application	provides user interface to lower levels
6 Presentation	provides data formatting and code conversion
5 Session	handles co-ordination between processes
4 Transport	provides control of quality of service
3 Network	sets up and maintains connections
2 Data Link	provides reliable data transfer between terminal and network
1 Physical	passes bit stream between terminal and network

The OSI layers... and their functions

Data Transmission

Digital information (1 or 0) is represented by two electrical voltage levels.

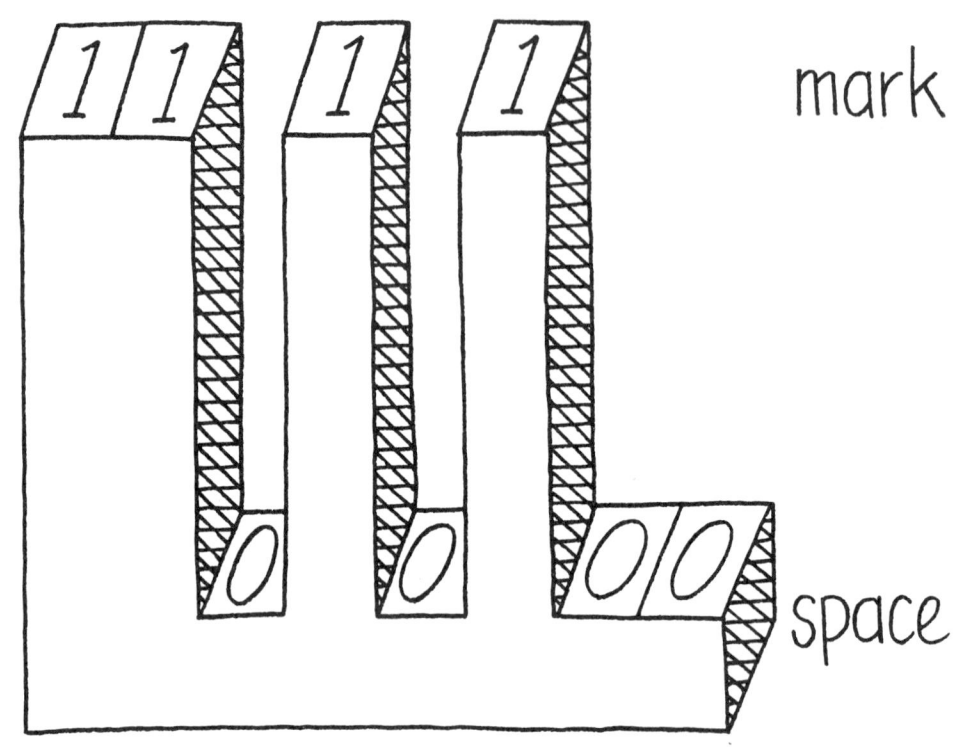

byte 1 1 0 1 0 1 0 0

With <u>serial</u> transmission the electrical signals representing the binary digits are sent sequentially over the same cable circuit.

Pulse Distortion by Transmission Lines

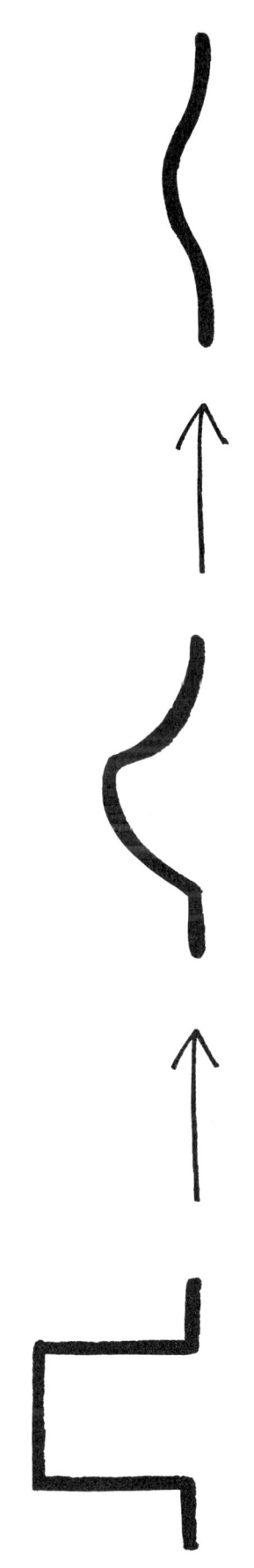

The longer the line, the greater the attenuation and distortion of the original pulse.

Effect of _repeating_ or _regenerating_ the signal:

Network Topologies

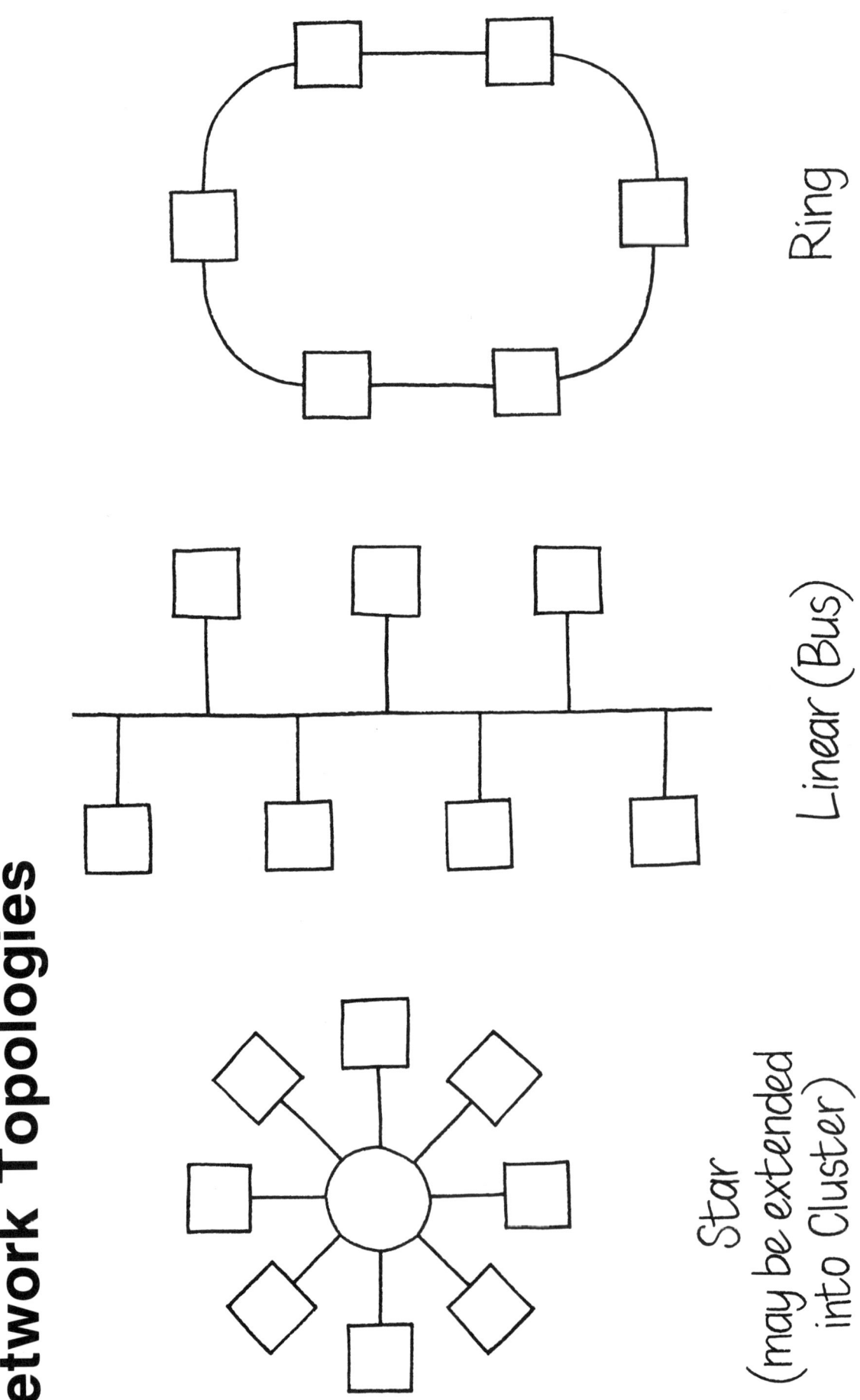

A Token Ring Network

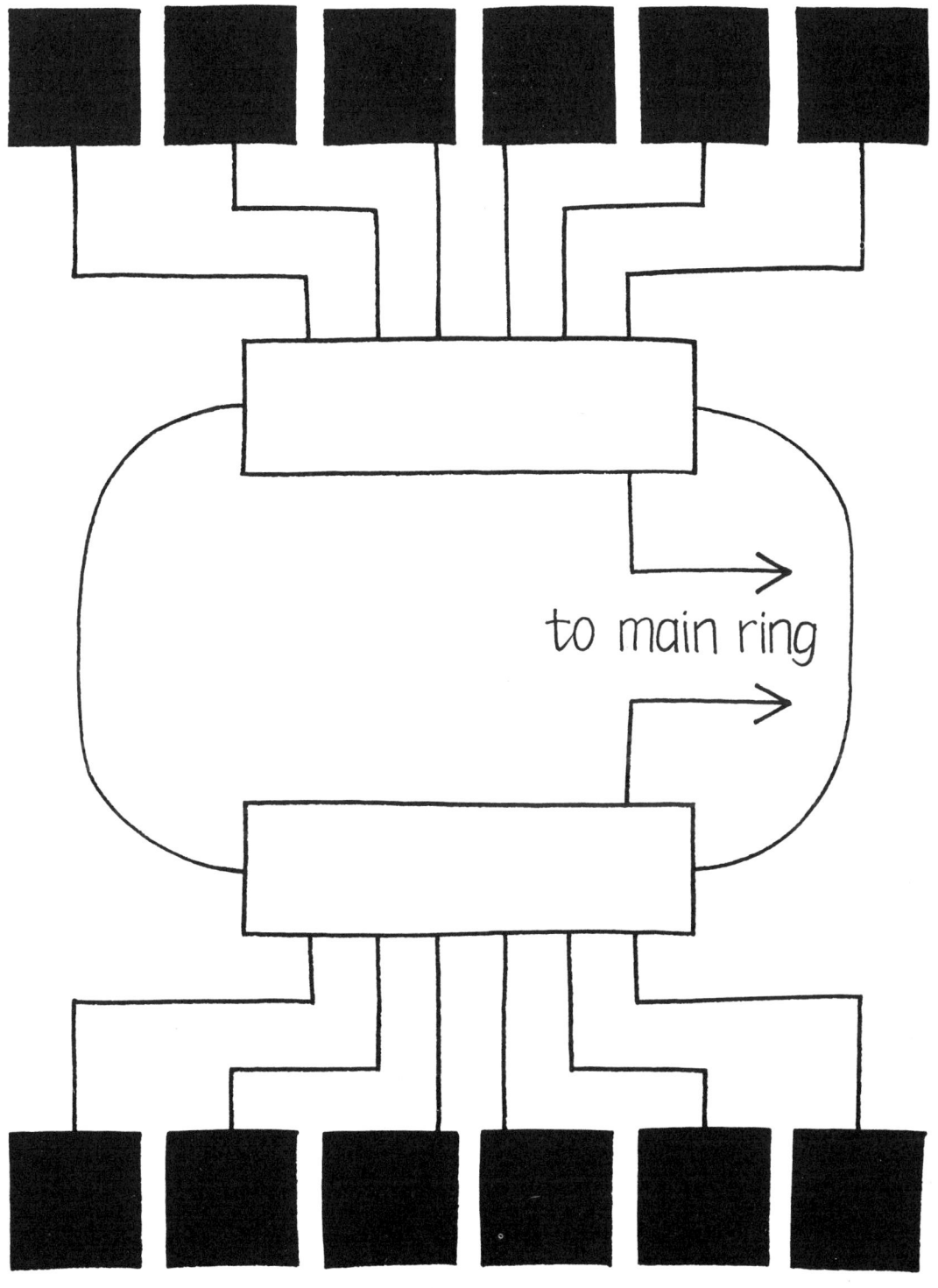

Datagrams

Any **LAN** can be viewed as a mechanism for transporting datagrams (loosely analogous to telegrams)

A **DATAGRAM** comprises

destination address	source address	data length	data	check digits

It features . . .
- one way communication
- carries both destination and source addresses
- variable length
- direct transmission (i.e. no call set-up/close down; no store and forward)

The Contention Problem

More than one station trying to transmit simultaneously

The same station being addressed by more than one station concurrently

Ethernet Approach – CSMA/CD

(**c**arrier **s**ense **m**ultiple **a**ccess with **c**ollision **d**etection)

Other stations sense when one is transmitting and wait for random period before retrying.

Problem: signal transmission takes finite time ~20cm per nanosecond. Hence possibility of two stations seizing line, believing it to be free.

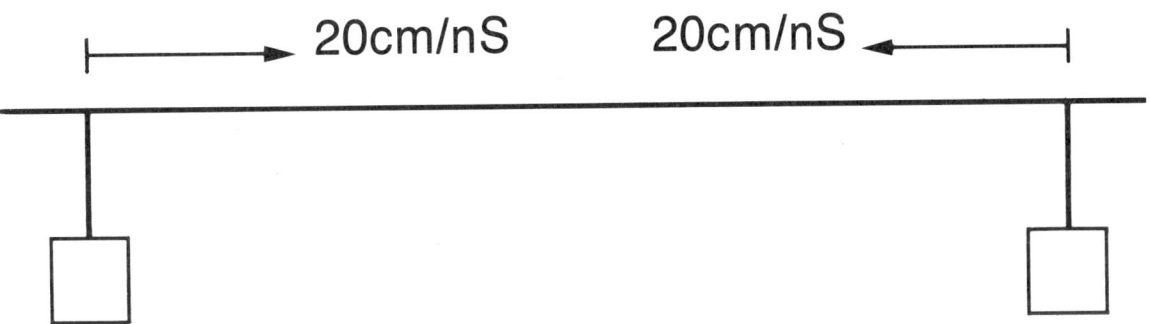

... hence need for collision detection

Ethernet Collision Detection

1 Network protocol requires that each transmitting station must receive from the destination point a copy of its transmission, and confirm that it is correct.

2 If check fails, collision detection hardware jams the line; all stations sense this and get off the line.

3 Stations are assigned random time intervals to wait before trying again.

4 If line jams again on restart, the range of delay intervals is increased automatically until successful restart is achieved.

Systems which avoid collision problems

Polling:
One station polling all the others in turn eliminates the possibility of collision, but is slow.

Token-passing:
A token is a form of electronic packet which passes repeatedly along a network; it is in essence a special purpose electronic message that says, "Here is permission to use the network."

When a station possesses the token, it possesses the network; other stations must wait until the token is passed.

The Token Ring Principle

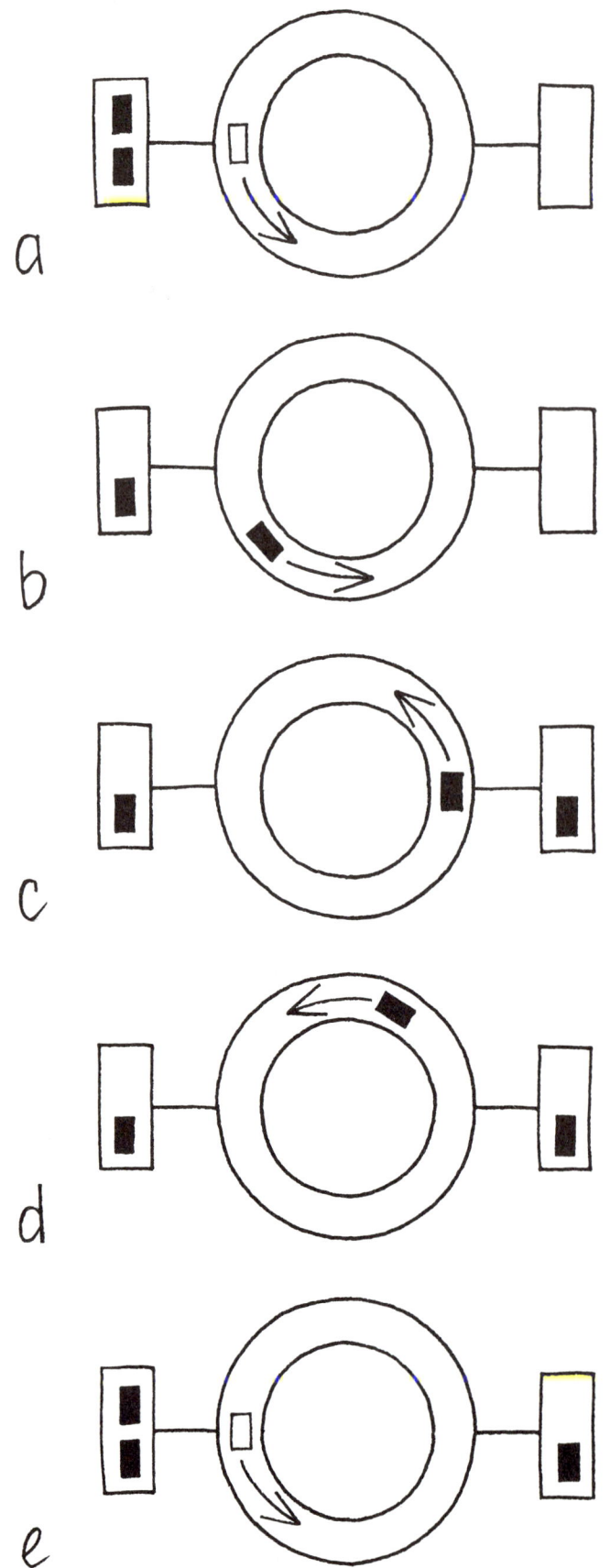

CHAPTER 8 | Applications software

The work presented in this chapter provides the opportunity to draw together most of the earlier work, and to integrate it with a broader curriculum if you so wish.

At the heart of it lies an accounts package, which is simple to set up and use, aimed at a level of accounting understanding which is likely to be suitable for many of the users of the Pupil's Book. Comprehensive instructions for installing the system are included in the student manual and will not be repeated here. However, we would emphasize one point: do not attempt to run the package from the disk on which it is supplied; copy it on to your students' working disks first.

The reason for this is that the batch file ACCOUNTS.BAT contains instructions which will run a program to set up the file FIRMDATA.DTA, if it does not exist. The program enables the user to place in that file his/her company name and address, registration and VAT numbers. As soon as this file is created, the program through which it was set up is destroyed. This means that you have close control over the companies which are set up, within a given student group. Each student involved can only set up one company, unless you give them another copy of the master disk, because the various accounts programs will not run without the file FIRMDATA.DTA being present.

The only hardware limitation which we anticipate is associated with the printer. Almost any 80 column or larger matrix printer should work, but the invoice preparation module outputs control codes to produce elongated and condensed mode printing and uses control codes appropriate to the Epson FX and LX series for these purposes. Most matrix printers use common (Epson) codes for print control, so this is not expected to cause any serious problems. Should you only have access to a daisywheel printer, then such variations in print style are obviously unavailable, and most daisywheel printers will simply ignore the codes, because they make no sense in the context of the range of signals these printers expect to receive.

Let us now look at the kind of activity which could involve students in the use of the accounts software and bring all the earlier learning into focus.

Suppose that each student, or pair of students, within a larger group are to set up companies which, in due course, will trade with one another. You will need to influence the choice of company activity fairly strongly to ensure that trade between companies is possible. For example, you may have several manufacturers (perhaps with two or three of them in competition over certain product ranges) and they are going to need both suppliers either of raw materials or of bought-out parts and purchasers of their finished goods. Perhaps the products are to be sold via third parties, e.g. retailers, or the producers might be selling direct to the end users. We are inclined to the view that the scene should be set around fairly small businesses, since it is easier to teach fundamental principles at this level.

And, of course, while some deal in products, others may deal in services, e.g. solicitors, architects, accountants, consulting engineers, quantity surveyors and a whole range of others. (What exactly do these people do? There is scope for careers work, contact with the local business organizations.) But whatever kinds of businesses are finally set up, you are going to need a couple of bankers. We suggest more than one, so that you can deal with the clearing process in due course (this allows much scope for dealing with the basics of banking).

The banks are, of course, the most likely source of capital when starting a business, but they are not going to lend without being convinced by a sound business plan that they should back a particular enterprise. This is not a business studies text, so we will not discuss the desirable content of a business plan further, other than to point out that a cash flow projection is a good and simple spreadsheet application. It could look something like the diagram below, but with the student choosing his/her own income and expenditure heads.

CASHFLOW (FORECAST & ACTUAL) FOR (YEAR)

	JANUARY		FEBRUARY		MARCH		APRIL		DECEMBER		12-MONTH TOTALS	
	BUDGET	ACTUAL	BUDGET	ACTUAL	BUDGET	ACTUAL	BUDGET	ACTUAL	BUDGET	ACTUAL	BUDGET	ACTUAL
:INCOME												
:PRODUCT 1 SALES	500		600		800						1900	0
:PRODUCT 2 SALES	200		500		800						1500	0
:SERVICES	250		300		200						750	0
:MISCELLANEOUS	50				100						150	0
											0	0
:TOTAL INCOME	1000	0	1400	0	1900	0	0		0	0	4300	0
:EXPENDITURE												
:PRINTING & STATIONERY	100				50						150	0
:TELEPHONE & POSTAGE	250		50		50						350	0
:TRADE CREDITORS	200		250		200						650	0
:SALARIES/WAGES INC NIC	1000		1000		1000						3000	0
:BANK CHARGES					50						50	0
:V.A.T.					500						500	0
											0	0
											0	0
:TOTAL EXPENDITURE	1550	0	1300	0	1850	0	0	0	0	0	4700	0
:INCOME - EXPENDITURE	-550	0	100	0	50	0		0	0	0	-400	0
:OPENING BANK BALANCE	2500	2500	1950	2500	2050	2500	210		2500	2100	2500	2500
:CLOSING BANK BALANCE	1950	2500	2050	2500	2100	2500		2500	2100	2500	2100	2500

When the banker agrees to finance a particular enterprise, a bank account has to be opened. You may wish to introduce a note of realism by undertaking work on check digits, if this has not already been covered, since a typical 8-figure account code is in fact a 7-figure code with a check digit. Transparencies dealing with a simple check digit system will be found in Appendix 1, Sequence FS3.

The terms of any bank loan or other banking services need to be negotiated – another good reason for having duplication of banks – and the banker will have to calculate interest and other charges on the agreed basis. S/he is also going to have to keep an eye on balances, to ensure that agreed credit limits are not exceeded. If a banker has some programming skill, s/he might wish to write specific software to deal with such problems, but an ability to handle files will be essential and it is doubtful if many users of an introductory text will have taken programming to this stage. So the majority will almost certainly use spreadsheet software as their main support in executing the various calculations involved.

If we turn for a moment to the accounting side of the business, which will be customers of the bank, perhaps the first module of background students require is on the application of VAT. There is frequently confusion between goods and services which are zero-rated (but which nevertheless are included in VAT returns) and those which are exempt and therefore not included in the returns. This distinction needs to be made.

Although there is currently a concession for small businesses, allowing payment of collected VAT to Customs and Excise to be postponed until it is actually received from the customer, our accounts system does not take advantage of this. The VAT due to Customs and Excise on each new transaction is added to the running total, when the invoice is generated. This enables a physical audit check to be performed, because the total VAT of all invoices with tax points in the period of the return must coincide with the VAT entry on the return. In order to get absolute accuracy, it is important to reset the VAT running totals promptly at the end of a return period.

A practical point on the generation of invoices: two copies are required, one for the customer and one for internal physical records. You may find it convenient to use 2-part plain continuous stationery for much of the accounts work. Even the cash flow spreadsheet needs two copies, one for the bank or another proposed source of capital and the other for internal records.

To minimize the paperwork and keep the system simple, we request payment against invoices and do not issue statements. Nor do we include an aged debtors listing, as you would expect in most commercial packages. However, in the reporting facilities, debtors are listed with invoice dates in chronological order, so on the scale of business we envisage, it is easy to pick out invoices for which payment is overdue.

Incidentally, many of the standard reports may be made either to output to screen or printer; some of those outputting to printer require more than 80 columns. But an 80-column matrix printer is adequate because condensed mode printing will allow 136 characters per line, which is more than enough. If this cannot be hardware set when required, you could run the command file TINYPRNT.COM, which is supplied on the accounts disk to send the standard ESC15 codes to the printer. (Turn the printer off and on again to revert to the default setting, i.e. normal print size.)

Another major module which students are going to require at an early stage is one dealing with salary and wages payments. There is no payroll module in the accounts package. We feel that a fully-fledged payroll module is too complex to be useful at this stage, and we suggest that the issue of statutory sick pay be left out altogether.

It may be of benefit for students to have access to tax and National Insurance Contributions (NIC) tables and to be shown how to use them in conjunction with P11 forms. Your local tax inspector may well be able to help with these, but failing that, we include a copy of form P11 as item V in Appendix 2, which could be photocopied. This is not the latest version of P11, but the more recent issue is too large for easy copying; it differs from its predecessor only on the NIC side and allows for more complex situations to be handled than we are going to require in the present exercise.

Although copies of tax and NIC tables would prove useful educational aids, you can do without them. So far as free pay is concerned, you may know that the annual free pay is related to an individual's tax code number by the expression;

annual free pay = tax code number * 10 + 9

and the weekly or monthly free pay grows uniformly towards this figure as the tax year goes on.

The tax levied on taxable pay will, of course, vary from budget to budget; all you need are the current rates and the taxable income bands to which they apply.

Similarly NIC payments due from both employee and employer are straight percentages applied to gross salary bands, and may vary according to the government from time to time.

It would not be unreasonable for students to build a spreadsheet to simulate the P11 transactions provided the salaries/wages are kept in the lowest tax band and a single NIC band. For a few students, you may wish to extend the exercise to cover gross salaries, spreading across more than one band. In such cases, the use of conditional statements will be necessary. There are several possible approaches to this extended exercise, but (using syntax appropriate to the software you have available) the suggestion in the diagrams opposite may be helpful. The upper diagram shows a possible spreadsheet, in which the range D4.F9 is infilled with current data at the start of a new tax year. The cells B11 and C11 are used for the individual's tax code number and letter respectively. The cells from row 16 onwards in column D are for the monthly gross pay entries; only one example entry has been made. All other cells, except month numbers, contain formulae, and these are illustrated opposite in the lower diagram. The notation used is that of Lotus 1–2–3; in case you are unfamiliar with this software, it may be useful to know that the information in curved brackets next to the cell reference applies to the cell format (in this case, a Fixed decimal point set to 2 places of decimals) and the information in square brackets refers to the cell width where it differs from the default value. With Lotus 1–2–3, all functions are preceded by the @ symbol, and references to absolute addresses include a $ sign before the column letter and row number. One may wish only the column reference to remain unchanged when a formula is copied (replicated) to other cells; in this case the $ precedes the column letter, but not the row number. This is exemplified in the lower diagram, cell L16, which refers in part to the address $G16.

TAX BAND DATA:

MONTHLY GROSS PAY		TAX RATE
UPPER LIMIT	LOWER LIMIT	
NONE	£3,435	60%
£3,434	£2,776	55%
£2,775	£2,118	50%
£2,117	£1,701	45%
£1,700	£1,493	40%
£1,492	£0	27%

} ROWS 4-9

TAX CODE 240L ← ROW 11

MONTH NO	PAY IN THE MONTH	TOTAL PAY PAY TO DATE	TOTAL FREE PAY TO DATE	TOTAL TAXABLE PAY TO DATE	TOTAL TAX DUE	TAX DEDUCTED	BAND 6	BAND 5	BAND 4	BAND 3	BAND 2	BAND 1	
1	2000.00	2000.00	200.75	1799.25	530.70	530.70	0.00	0.00	0.00	99.25	208.00	1492.00	← ROW 16
2		2000.00	401.50	1598.50	445.44	85.26 R	0.00	0.00	0.00	0.00	106.50	1492.00	← ROW 18
3		2000.00	602.25	1397.75	377.39	68.05 R	0.00	0.00	0.00	0.00	0.00	1397.75	← ROW 20
4		2000.00	803.00	1197.00	323.19	54.20 R	0.00	0.00	0.00	0.00	0.00	1197.00	
5		2000.00	1003.75	996.25	268.99	54.20 R	0.00	0.00	0.00	0.00	0.00	996.25	
6		2000.00	1204.50	795.50	214.79	54.20 R	0.00	0.00	0.00	0.00	0.00	795.50	
7		2000.00	1405.25	594.75	160.58	54.20 R	0.00	0.00	0.00	0.00	0.00	594.75	
8		2000.00	1606.00	394.00	106.38	54.20 R	0.00	0.00	0.00	0.00	0.00	394.00	
9		2000.00	1806.75	193.25	52.18	54.20 R	0.00	0.00	0.00	0.00	0.00	193.25	
10		2000.00	2007.50	0.00	0.00	52.18 R	0.00	0.00	0.00	0.00	0.00	0.00	
11		2000.00	2208.25	0.00	0.00	0.00	0.00	0.00	0.00	0.00	0.00	0.00	
12		2000.00	2409.00	0.00	0.00	0.00	0.00	0.00	0.00	0.00	0.00	0.00	
↑ B	↑ D	↑ E	↑ F	↑ G	↑ H	↑ I ↑ J	↑ K	↑ L	↑ M	↑ N	↑ O	↑ P	← COLUMN IDENTIFIERS

```
E16:  (F2) [W14] +D16
F16:  (F2) [W14] ($B$11*10+9)/12*B16
G16:  (F2) [W14] @IF(F16>E16,0,E16-F16)
H16:  (F2) +$F$4*K16+$F$5*L16+$F$6*M16+$F$7*N16+$F$8*O16+$F$9*P16
I16:  (F2) @IF(H16<0,0,@ABS(H16))
K16:  (F2) @IF(G16>$D$5,G16,0)
L16:  (F2) @IF(K16<>0,$D$5-$E$5+1,@IF($G16>$D$6,$G16-$D$6,0))
M16:  (F2) @IF(L16<>0,$D$6-$E$6+1,@IF($G16>$D$7,$G16-$D$7,0))
N16:  (F2) @IF(M16<>0,$D$7-$E$7+1,@IF($G16>$D$8,$G16-$D$8,0))
O16:  (F2) @IF(N16<>0,$D$8-$E$8+1,@IF($G16>$D$9,$G16-$D$9,0))
P16:  (F2) @IF(O16<>0,$D$9-$E$9,$G16)
E18:  (F2) [W14] +D18+E16
F18:  (F2) [W14] ($B$11*10+9)/12*B18
G18:  (F2) [W14] @IF(F18>E18,0,E18-F18)
H18:  (F2) +$F$4*K18+$F$5*L18+$F$6*M18+$F$7*N18+$F$8*O18+$F$9*P18
I18:  (F2) @IF(H18<0,0,@ABS(H18-H16))
J18:  [W1] @IF(H16>H18,"R","")
K18:  (F2) @IF(G18>$D$5,G18,0)
L18:  (F2) @IF(K18<>0,$D$5-$E$5+1,@IF($G18>$D$6,$G18-$D$6,0))
M18:  (F2) @IF(L18<>0,$D$6-$E$6+1,@IF($G18>$D$7,$G18-$D$7,0))
N18:  (F2) @IF(M18<>0,$D$7-$E$7+1,@IF($G18>$D$8,$G18-$D$8,0))
O18:  (F2) @IF(N18<>0,$D$8-$E$8+1,@IF($G18>$D$9,$G18-$D$9,0))
P18:  (F2) @IF(O18<>0,$D$9-$E$9,$G18)
E20:  (F2) [W14] +D20+E18
F20:  (F2) [W14] ($B$11*10+9)/12*B20
G20:  (F2) [W14] @IF(F20>E20,0,E20-F20)
H20:  (F2) +$F$4*K20+$F$5*L20+$F$6*M20+$F$7*N20+$F$8*O20+$F$9*P20
I20:  (F2) @IF(H20<0,0,@ABS(H20-H18))
J20:  [W1] @IF(H18>H20,"R","")
K20:  (F2) @IF(G20>$D$5,G20,0)
L20:  (F2) @IF(K20<>0,$D$5-$E$5+1,@IF($G20>$D$6,$G20-$D$6,0))
M20:  (F2) @IF(L20<>0,$D$6-$E$6+1,@IF($G20>$D$7,$G20-$D$7,0))
N20:  (F2) @IF(M20<>0,$D$7-$E$7+1,@IF($G20>$D$8,$G20-$D$8,0))
O20:  (F2) @IF(N20<>0,$D$8-$E$8+1,@IF($G20>$D$9,$G20-$D$9,0))
P20:  (F2) @IF(O20<>0,$D$9-$E$9,$G20)
```

The lower diagram on page 163 shows only a limited range of cell contents, but sufficient to set the pattern for subsequent rows. Note that the entries for month 1 (row 16) are in some columns different from the entries in subsequent rows.

This spreadsheet will not cover all eventualities, for example, a change of code part way through the year or a 'month 1' situation. It could be modified to do so, but not with students on an introductory course. In fact, only the more able will cope with the nested 'if' statements in cells like L16. It may be helpful if an example statement is presented first in plain English with a structured layout something like:

> IF contents of cell K16 are not zero
> THEN display the result of subtracting the contents of D6 from the contents of D5
> ELSE
> > IF contents of G16 are greater than the contents of D6
> > THEN display the result of subtracting the contents of D6 from the contents of G16
> > ELSE display the value zero.

The third teaching module, which is going to be essential before students can handle their accounts sensibly is one in which simple cash-book record keeping is covered. The software provided requires both income and expenditure entries to be posted to appropriate account heads at the time of entry. So account heads must be set up before any transactions can be entered in the system. From this point on, students should be able to cope.

Apart from the financial aspects of setting up and running a business, which we have dwelt on so far, there are obvious opportunities for using word processing and database software.

For example, a firm might wish to keep all customer or potential customer details on a database, which could include a field for indicating the range of products likely to be of interest to the customer, date fields indicating when he last did business with the firm and when the last contact (e.g. by direct mail) was made.

With this data available, one could extract all records of people who have never yet bought from the firm, or who have not been contacted within the last four months or who have an interest in a particular product range. The possibilities are almost endless.

Depending on the software your students are using, there is a strong possibility that the extracted data could be output to an ASCII file on disk instead of a printer; most word processing packages can handle non-document ASCII data files in mailmerge operations and you may wish to take appropriate students rather further than Chapter 5 of the student text, so that they could originate a mailshot personally addressed to each of a selected group of customers. This would provide a chance to introduce some basic ideas on marketing.

To summarize:

1 The first part of Chapter 8 enables students to integrate all the work they have covered in previous chapters and to use a fairly substantial applications package.
2 By selecting the participants for specific activity units within the

overall project, you are able to bring together small groups of individuals of comparable ability and take them rather further than the work covered in earlier chapters of the book.
3 You have the opportunity to integrate the project with some careers work, should you so wish.
4 There is also an opportunity, which is almost a necessity, to integrate closely with other business studies teaching, though this need not be computer-related.

If this enterprise project is to be treated seriously, it should extend over several months, if at all possible. There should be monthly bank statements and the accountant in each organization will be required to reconcile the computer-held transaction records with balances on the bank statement. The bank statements should, of course, include bank charges and interest, if appropriate, once a quarter.

Rates and rent could be paid by standing order or direct debit (more business studies teaching) and appropriate standing order or direct debit *pro formas* could be prepared under word processing software.

Accuracy of input is obviously of great importance when handling an accounts system, and you may wish to use Transparency sequence 8.1, to illustrate the concept of using document batching with control slips, as a means of ensuring tht input is accurate.

To assist with bank reconciliation, the software reports module offers a totalling facility for individual transactions which were combined and entered on one paying-in slip, when it lists to screen the details of income for a specified month. A parallel facility is offered on the expenditure side, for cheques paid in respect of more than one invoice. By requesting output to printer, a slightly more detailed listing of income and expenditure can be obtained for any specified month or for all months, from the start of the financial year.

The other major reporting facility is analysis of income and expenditure by account head. This might be for the year to date (and ultimately for the full year) but it can be restricted to a specified date band, thus making it a suitable vehicle for determining 'actual' values, to insert on the cash flow spreadsheet. One may also wish at times to restrict reporting to specific account heads and this facility is also available.

The last section of Chapter 8 deals with some aspects of programming, skirting, where possible, around specific syntax references, which vary from one dialect to another of BASIC. It starts with a brief discussion of language levels and the need for assemblers, compilers or interpreters, which revises and enlarges slightly on work touched on in Chapter 3. You may wish to refer again to Transparency sequences 3.1.2, 3.1.4, 3.1.5. Afterwards, we are into programming concepts illustrated in BASIC.

We believe that coding and the rudiments of program construction can be taught in parallel. For example, a program with this algorithm:
- ☐ Clear screen.
- ☐ Display prompt 'What is your name?'.

☐ Take in keyboard response and assign it to variable N$.
☐ Clear screen.
☐ Display as output 'Hello, (input name)'.

introduces: key words CLS, print, input;
the syntax for string variable identifiers;
the outputting of a literal and a variable value in a common print statement.

The program may subsequently be modified to display the same output not once, but 20 times, one under the other, and by so doing we have added the standard FOR... NEXT reserved words to the student's vocabulary, together with the construct for defined iteration. Whilst dealing with simple *definite loops*, one could take appropriate students into the idea of *nested loops*. Specify that you want each successive line of 'Hello, (input name)' to be indented two spaces further than the previous line. You will have to explain that print statements ending with a semicolon retain the cursor at the end of the last thing printed; but this is the only new syntax required. After that, it remains only to be encouraging as students grope towards the idea of nested loops along the lines:

```
FOR N = 1 TO 20
    PRINT "Hello",; n$
    FOR p = 1 TO N
    PRINT "";
    NEXT p
NEXT N
```

Students generally enjoy producing audible output, and this could be a vehicle for introducing conditional statements into this very simple introductory work, by including in the outer loop a statement such as

IF N = 10 THEN PRINT CHR$(7);

It introduces another key-word and recalls earlier work on ASCII codes.

Obviously more complex examples of both definite loops involving the full statement for n = a TO b STEP c where a,b, c are integers, and conditional statements involving the ELSE clause (and probably logical connectives) must come later. But we favour introducing new concepts with the simplest possible syntax and the building on them as and when the need arises.

We find the construction of simple menu-driven software provides opportunities for teaching basic principles. It will, for example:

1 Introduce a post-condition indefinite iteration.
2 Encourage students to consider and produce attractive and easily read screen layouts.
3 Require students to design programs which will validate simple inputs.
4 Introduce the concept of routing to sub-routines or procedures.

It has the additional advantage that it can be used in an extended exercise which produces a useful program.

A worksheet is given at the end of this chapter. Initially, only page 1 of this should be given to students. When this task has been satisfactorily completed, pages 2 and 3 reveal a wider scene and show how the initial work is to be incorporated in it.

We have tried to leave enough 'unsaid' to make the project interesting for reasonably able students, but conversely this means that the less able are going to require a fair amount of tutorial support. At the end of Chapter 8 in the student text there are two other assignment suggestions. The first is quite straightforward but note the need for the student to know more about print formatting than they have up to this point. The handling of this will depend on the interpreter, but we have in mind statements like the GWBASIC PRINT USING "##.##" for a four figure output including a decimal point and two decimal places. The student will also need to know about INKEY$, in order that a spacebar (and *only* the spacebar) depression may be used to return to the opening menu.

The second assignment is quite useful in that it makes quite heavy demands on the student's ability to control both screen and printed output. There is also ample scope for individual students to introduce their own variants.

A final point: you will notice that we have in illustrative material always taken in numerical inputs as strings, converting them to values for calculation purposes only when we have checked that they are valid numbers.

With BASIC, if you assign an accidentally non-numerical value from the keyboard to a numeric variable identifier, you get nothing worse than a ?REDO FROM START error message; but with some other languages, the program may abort. Either way, the possibility is best avoided by taking in the input as a string and subsequently finding if it is valid.

Sample worksheet

Unit conversion software

Write a program which will cause the screen shown below to be displayed.

```
                UNIT CONVERSION SOFTWARE
    to be used for converting from metric to Imperial units
                        and vice versa
            Please select. . .
            1  to convert from metric to Imperial
            2  to convert from Imperial to metric
            3  to exit from the program
            Enter 1, 2 or 3 and press ⟨ENTER⟩ . . .
```

It must accept the user's input only if it is valid – i.e. it must be 1, 2 or 3. Any other input must be erased and the cursor repositioned ready for the corrected input.

To do this, you need to confirm that the input is only one character long (use the function LEN(varname) to determine this). If it passes this test, check that its value is in the specified range. You may wish to know that the ASCII code for the character 1 is 49 (decimal); for the character 2 it is 50 and for 3 it is 51. The function ASC(N$) returns the ASCII code of the first character of the string represented by N$, so for the input to be valid, we are testing to see if ASC(varname) lies in the range 49 to 51.

If it passes this test, print a message at the foot of the screen:

    YOU HAVE SELECTED OPTION . . .

            [chosen option number to be displayed here.]

Optionally, you may activate the BEL (PRINT CHR$(7);) in the event of an unacceptable input.

In order to make the message 'YOU HAVE SELECTED OPTION n' appear at the bottom of the screen when a valid input is selected, you had either to use several IF . . . . THEN . . . statements, or if your BASIC interpreter allowed it, a CASE statement.

Modify these statements now so that instead of displaying a message on the screen, you route the user to an appropriate second-level menu as shown in the screen below and the screen on the next worksheet. The statements to display these menus and validate the input of option choice will be similar to those you have already used for the first-level menu. To keep each menu (including the first one you have already designed) in a self-contained tidy unit, we shall place them in *sub-routines* or *procedures* (most BASIC interpreters use sub-routines, but some use procedures).

Your first menu will now be called from a very short main program with the sample statement:

    GOSUB 1000 'Where the top level menu routine begins.

and if the contents of subroutine 1000 are within a post-condition loop thus:

    REPEAT
       |
       |
    UNTIL OPTION$="3" 'assuming OPTION$ to be the variable name assigned to the user input in subroutine 1000.

control will not return to the main program until the user calls option 3 of the main menu to exit from the program.

If REPEAT . . . . UNTIL is not available in your BASIC, then the same effect must be produced using either the conditional statement IF . . . THEN . . . with GOTO, or WHILE. . . WEND, with an additional statement before the loop, to ensure that it is run at least once.

CONVERSION FROM METRIC TO IMPERIAL UNITS
AVAILABLE OPTIONS:

    1 kilometres to miles
    2 kilogrammes to pounds
    3 litres to gallons
    4 return to top-level menu

    Enter 1–4 and press ⟨ENTER⟩ . . .

```
CONVERSION FROM IMPERIAL TO METRIC UNITS
            AVAILABLE OPTIONS:
              1  miles to kilometres
              2  pounds to kilogrammes
              3  gallons to litres
              4  return to top-level menu
            Enter 1-4 and press ⟨ENTER⟩ ...
```

In the same way that the subroutine 1000 keeps refreshing the call on the main (top-level) menu until option 3 is chosen, so each of the subsidiary level menus must also be refreshed.

When an option in the range 1–3 is chosen from either of the second-level menus, a new input screen should be displayed having the form:

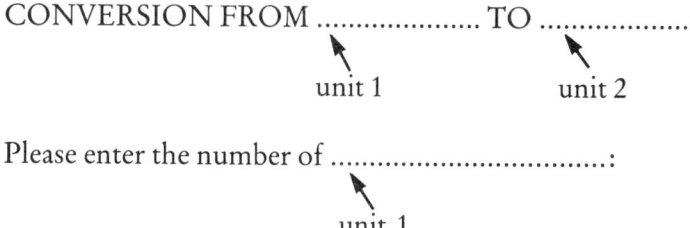

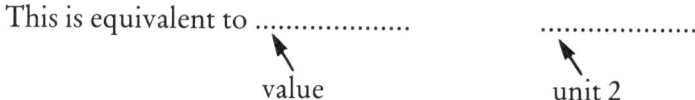

As soon as the user has entered the number which is to be converted, a further line should appear on the screen:

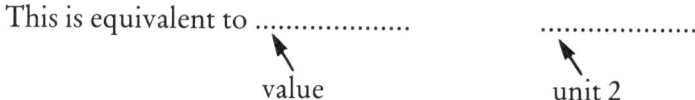

You could save yourself some work if you used the six subroutines corresponding to the six possible options from the second-level menus to set values used in a single subroutine which all six subroutines could call on.

The constants you require are:
     0.612 miles is the same as 1 kilometre
     2.205 pounds is the same as 1 kilogramme
     0.220 gallons is the same as 1 litre

REMEMBER: – plan your program before you code it!

Chapter 8 – Transparency sequence 1
Input data controls

Notes

Transparency reference	8.1.1	We can never be certain that variable data is without error – at best we can only check that it lies within defined limits of expectation. What we can ensure is that immediately after the originator has entered data on a data input form, control procedures are implemented which will trap as many errors as possible from that point on.
	8.1.2	This transparency provides an example of input data control, based on sales data received by telephone. The foil is divided horizontally and will be best handled by a progressive revelation technique. It makes reference to a number of terms which will require further explanation – *control slip* and *control data* in particular, are likely to be terms students have not met before. These are explained on the next transparency.
	8.1.3	This describes typical control data and the way in which the computer is programmed to undertake the same control counts and calculations as those undertaken by the Data Control Section staff. Any discrepancy between control slip figures and computer calculations will inhibit the filing of data on the computer system, for the form or batch of forms where an error has occurred.
		The term *hash total* is used here; the term is explained on the next transparency.
	8.1.4	This presents an example of a hash total based on a hardware order. The summation of the entries under the 'quantity' head has no physical significance, but if the total calculated by the computer at the time of input, agrees with the total prepared by the Data Control Clerk, there is a strong likelihood that this important data has been input correctly.
		Note that the check cannot ensure 100% accuracy of input data. For example, quantities could be transposed; the order could have been entered as requiring 10 gross of screws and 5 pairs of hinges. The hash total would still have been right.
		At the end of the day, there is no substitute for great care, concentration and accuracy. But people tend to be less than perfect and a good input data control system helps to compensate for the short-comings of personnel.

Principles of Input Data Control

1. The fewer manual processes the data passes through, the smaller the chance of error. (Hence an advantage of direct hand print recognition systems)

2. Control and the building in of data validation checks must be the first process after data capture.

Input Data Control Example

Organizational Unit	Function	Data Control Activity
Sales Department	Telephone sales; accepts sales orders	Data transcribed to serially numbered data input forms
Data Control Section	Devise and implement systems to ensure data integrity	1 Ensure that all serial numbers are accounted for 2 Batch order data input forms; prepare control slips
Data Preparation Section	Prepare data for input to computer (e.g. key to disk)	Control slip data input to computer in addition to the prime data

Use of Control Data

Data normally recorded on a control slip comprises
- number of forms in the batch
- hash totals for individual forms
- hash total for batch

Data input software is designed to perform the same count and the same totalling.
It then compares the results of its computation with the control slip data (input along with the prime data).

If comparison is not exact, the data is not filed; the batch must be checked and reinput.

Hash Total

The hash total has no meaning or value in itself but it is used for checking purposes.

For example:

Qty	Units	Description
5	gross	1in. × No. 8 steel screws
10	pairs	2in. steel hinges
4	sheets	8ft. × 4ft. 10mm plywood
1	kg	1½in. nails

The hash total for this order form would be:
5 + 10 + 4 + 1 i.e. 20

Appendix 1

Transparency sequence FS1
Disk handling

Notes

Transparency reference

FS1.1 and FS1.5 appear over three pages in this manual and will need photocopying individually before being made into transparencies.

FS1.1 This is of relevance if students are using 5¼ inch diskettes, but of much less importance if 3½ inch diskettes are being used, since the window will normally be covered by the spring-loaded shutter.

FS1.2 Similarly, this transparency is of much more relevance to 5¼ inch disk users because the 3½ inch disks are so much more robust. If it is used, it may be worth pointing out that if a diskette falls from the edge of a desk, it is usually less damaging to let it fall than it is to try to save it by grabbing it on the way down.

FS1.3 to FS1.5 These three transparencies are relevant regardless of the diskette size and type. Note the proviso in FS1.5 regarding the insertion of diskettes before switching a computer on. We regard this procedure as bad practice, generally speaking, but occasionally you will come across systems where the handbook specifically states that the diskette should be inserted before switching on. Hence the proviso.

Transparency sequence FS2
Systems-related transparencies

You may wish to come back to different parts of this sequence at different stages in a course. We have tended to minimize systems work in the student text, since the prime purpose of the book is to help readers get to grips with general purpose applications software. Only essential system commands have been covered.

In our view, some additional systems background is desirable, but it probably needs to be injected in very small units, as it becomes necessary. It is for this reason that we suggest that you peruse the material in this free-standing sequence and dip into it at different times.

Notes

Transparency reference

FS2.1 An introductory transparency which illustrates the point that a complete system comprises both hardware and software. This could be used at a very early stage, for on the hardware side it could link into Sequence 2.1, if you wish to use it this way.

Our own preference, however, is to use it as a revision of hardware terms and functions, but more importantly as a lead-in to software and systems software in particular.

FS2.2 This is almost an aside, but as soon as one introduces the terms software and hardware, it may be useful to provide concise definitions of these terms. If one is going on to deal with the loading of the operating system, one needs to talk about instructions resident in *firmware*. Hence the definition of firmware on the same transparency.

FS2.3   If one were to follow the hardware route for a moment, this group of overlays may be helpful.

FS2.3a   This takes basically the same form as the corresponding diagram in Sequence 2.1, but now the contents of the processor and memory boxes are revealed in rather more detail. Within the processor, the important units at this stage are the control unit and the ALU (arithmetic and logic unit).

FS2.3b   The first overlay, should be made in a contrasting colour if possible; its purpose is to illustrate the definition of the CPU (central processing unit) as including both the processor and local memory. You may wish to define a microprocessor at this time (all the shaded portions formed on one chip).

FS2.3c   The second overlay gives the opportunity to use the terms *secondary* storage or *auxiliary* storage which are used interchangeably by various examining bodies. It should be pointed out that the control unit, under instruction from programs, governs the transfer of data between memory and secondary storage.

FS2.4   Back on the software route. This transparency is used to describe briefly the broad purpose of utility programs and compilers/interpreters; then to concentrate on the operating system. One may reuse this transparency, if it is decided to pursue the other systems software at a later stage.

FS2.5   This is a consciously limited statement of the purpose of an operating system, which should be sufficient for a first encounter. FS2.10 gives a much fuller statement and may be useful at a later stage if one employs the technique of 'diminishing deception'. The only point on FS2.5 which may merit further comment is the reference to the 'theoretical' portability of software.

This is because some systems nominally running the same operating system may have some hardware variations such as dedicated keys and software designed to be run on such systems may well have been tailored to take advantage of these dedicated functions. Such software may well not run on a system without these facilities. There are also some systems claiming to be IBM compatible, which are nearly so, but not quite. This occasionally leads to software installation problems.

FS2.6   This transparency, in addition to classifying applications software as either dedicated to a specific purpose or general purpose, indicates that the loading of the operating system must precede the loading of any application software.

FS2.7   This transparency may be needed much earlier. It depends on the way you have approached the work, as to whether it retains its position in this sequence or is placed elsewhere.

It should be explained that .DAT is not a standard extension (.DTA is also widely used) but some meaningful extension should be used to indicate a data file. Other widely used extensions are .DOC for a document file and .LTR for standard letters.

If you wish to extend the work at this time you could, for example, point out that most implementations of BASIC and Pascal automatically add the extensions .BAS and .PAS respectively to the source code files.

The importance of .COM and .EXE files, as being the only files containing machine-readable code should be stressed. These are the only files (other than batch files, that simply list system commands or executable files) which can be run by entering the file name at the system prompt.

FS2.8a–e A family of overlays to illustrate the loading of many operating systems. Some, such as the Acorn A (Archimedes) series carry the entire operating system (and a BASIC interpreter) in an unusually large ROM of 512K and in this case the family of transparencies would be inappropriate. But for quite a while yet, the standard business micro technique of loading the majority of the system from disk into RAM will persist.

The transparencies make reference to the major functions of the operating system, as supervising all input/output and controlling the disk operating system.

FS2.9 This transparency says a little more about the outer layer in the previous set of overlays.

Points which may be worth making:
1 That there are some direct commands, e.g. DIR, COPY etc. (in PCDOS/MSDOS) – more about those in subsequent slides.
2 That COMMAND.COM is not in direct command when another command file has been loaded. How many times have you had a student working with, say, WordStar try to change the logged drive by entering A: instead of using the WordStar command L to initiate a change of logged drive?

FS2.10 Mentioned in FS2.5 above as a fuller exposition of the functions of an operating system. One of those functions is the provision of a range of internal commands, and this leads naturally to FS2.11.

FS2.11 Distinguishes between internal and external commands. A common student mistake is to believe that an external command can be used without logging on to the disk or directory which contains the appropriate utility command file.

It is certainly worthwhile going on to two further transparencies at this stage, one giving some examples of internal commands, the other of external commands. We have not provided master sheets for these, because they will vary depending both on the operating system being used and on the point that free-standing module is introduced. We suggest as a minimum, commands which will:

1 List the directory of a disk to screen or printer.
2 Enable the copying of files from one disk to another or from one name to another on the same disk.
3 Delete a file.
4 Show the use of wildcards in all these operations (in the case of MSDOS/PCDOS all these will be internal commands).
5 Format a floppy disk.
6 Make an exact copy of a floppy disk.
7 Check the status of a disk and memory (as examples of external commands).

If a hard disk is available to students, you may wish also to include BACKUP and RESTORE.

Of course there are other useful utilities, but we feel these are the most essential for anyone working through an introductory text.

Transparency sequence FS3
Check digits

It must be emphasized that there are many different check digit systems. For the purpose of this example, we have chosen a very simple but effective system. If you wish to take this work further, you might like to ask a mail order company what check digit system they apply to their catalogue numbers and illustrate that system by reference to specific catalogue items.

Notes

Transparency FS3a–c

FS3a–c appear on one page in this manual and you will need to mask the areas shown to make the individual transparencies.

This 3-stage sequence illustrates a modulus 11 check digit system in which the multiplying constants are 1, 2, 3, 4, 5, 6. FS3a appears in bold type, FS3b is in light type and FS3c is in capitals for easy reference.

Any single digit constants may be used; for example, one mail order company uses 1, 3, 7, 1, 3, 7.

Having illustrated how check digits are determined, why not transpose two figures in the stock number (a common inputting error) and show that the check digit traps the error?

How to handle floppy disks –

DON'T HANDLE THEM

... except by the edge where the labels are.

The active surface may be damaged by

- fingerprints
- coffee spills
- dust
- cigarette ash
- even sneezes!!

... so keep the disk in its sleeve when not in use.

AVOID MECHANICAL DAMAGE

Don't bend them
 drop things on them
 or otherwise mistreat them
  (which you will if you leave
   them lying around)

<u>Do</u> store them flat and not under pressure.

BEWARE MAGNETIC FIELDS

Data and programs are coded and the code stored on disk in the form of magnetic patterns.

An extraneous magnetic field could affect this pattern and corrupt your data!

Unwanted magnetic fields come from equipment, such as:

* television sets

* electric motors running fans, typewriters, etc.

* unscreened mains transformers

* telephone hand-set

AVOID EXTREMES OF TEMPERATURE

10°C - 50°C is acceptable - outside this range, the strength of the magnetic patterns on the disk may weaken. If it is comfortable enough for you to work, it is OK for the disks.

How to load floppy disks - **GENTLY!**
Don't force them into the disk drives.
- ease them in gently to avoid bending the jacket or scratching the disk
Don't insert them before switching the equipment on (unless specifically instructed otherwise)
- switching transients may corrupt file contents
Remember to close the latch (if there is one) after insertion.

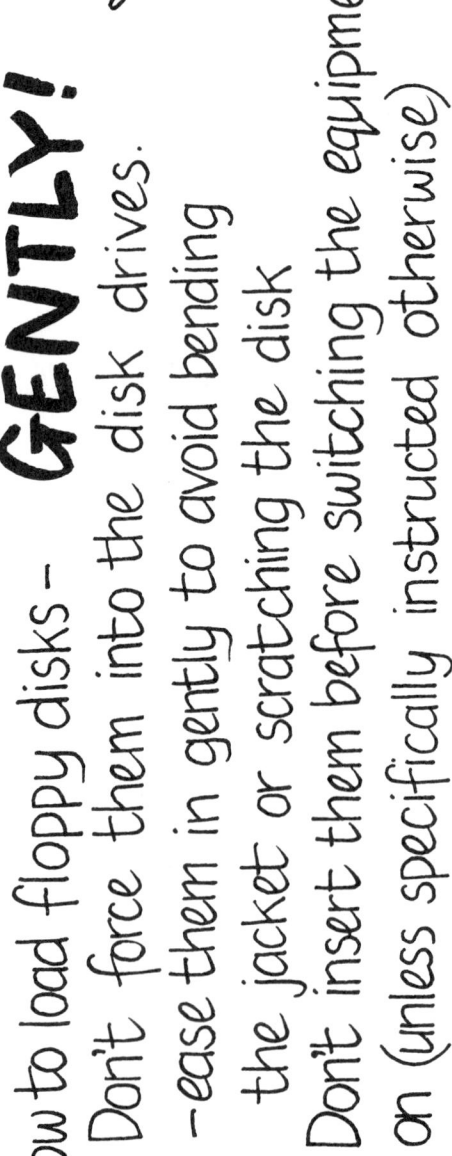

A Computer System

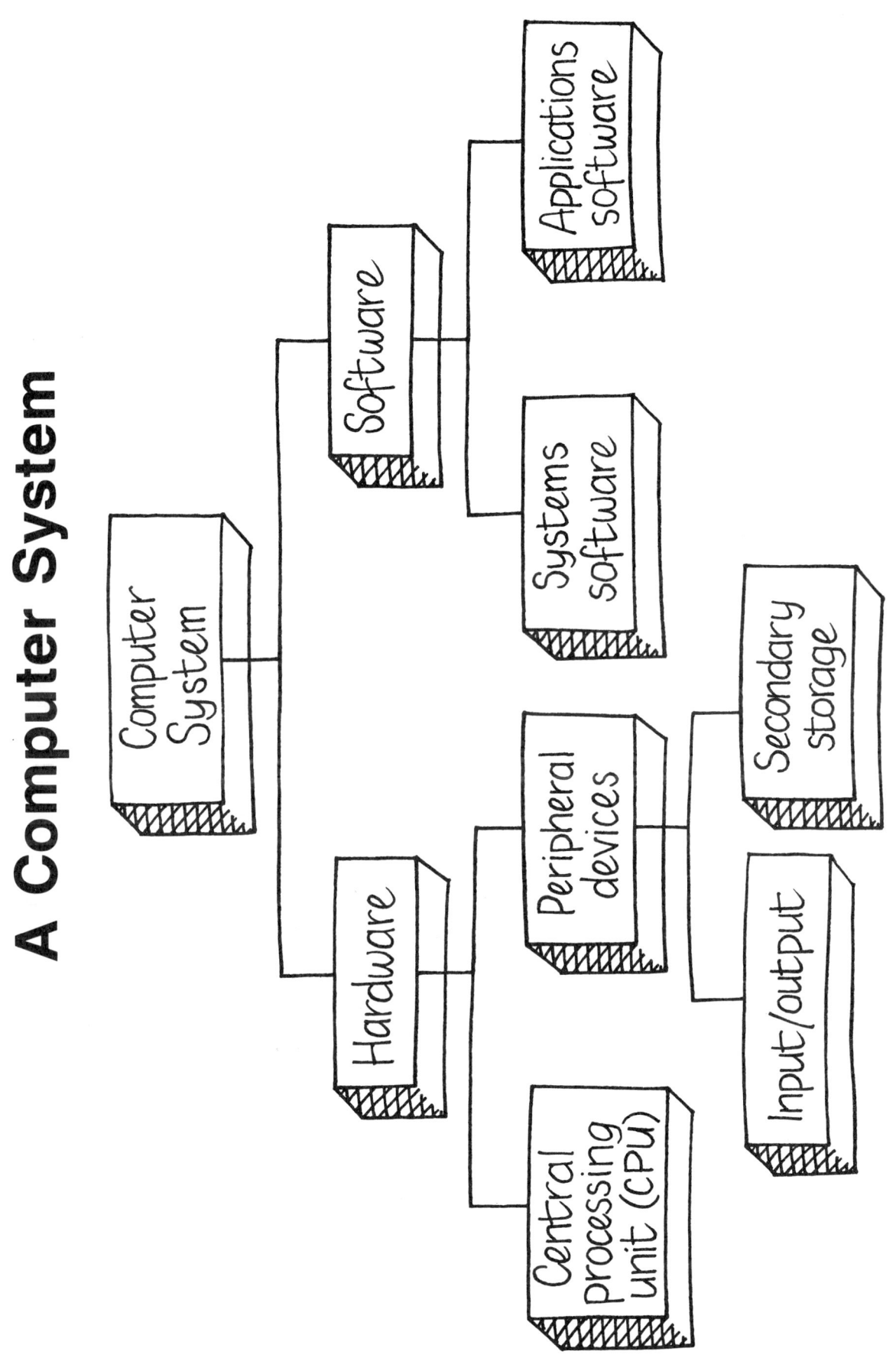

Software – the general term for all computer programs which can be run on computer hardware.

Hardware – the physical computer and peripherals (e.g. printers, plotters, VDUs, analogue to digital convertors, etc) including all electronic circuitry.

Firmware – a program permanently held in a 'read only memory' (**ROM**) chip. Sometimes an application program may be 'blown' into firmware, but usually only programs which manage the computer's internal operations are held in this way.

A Detailed Computer Model

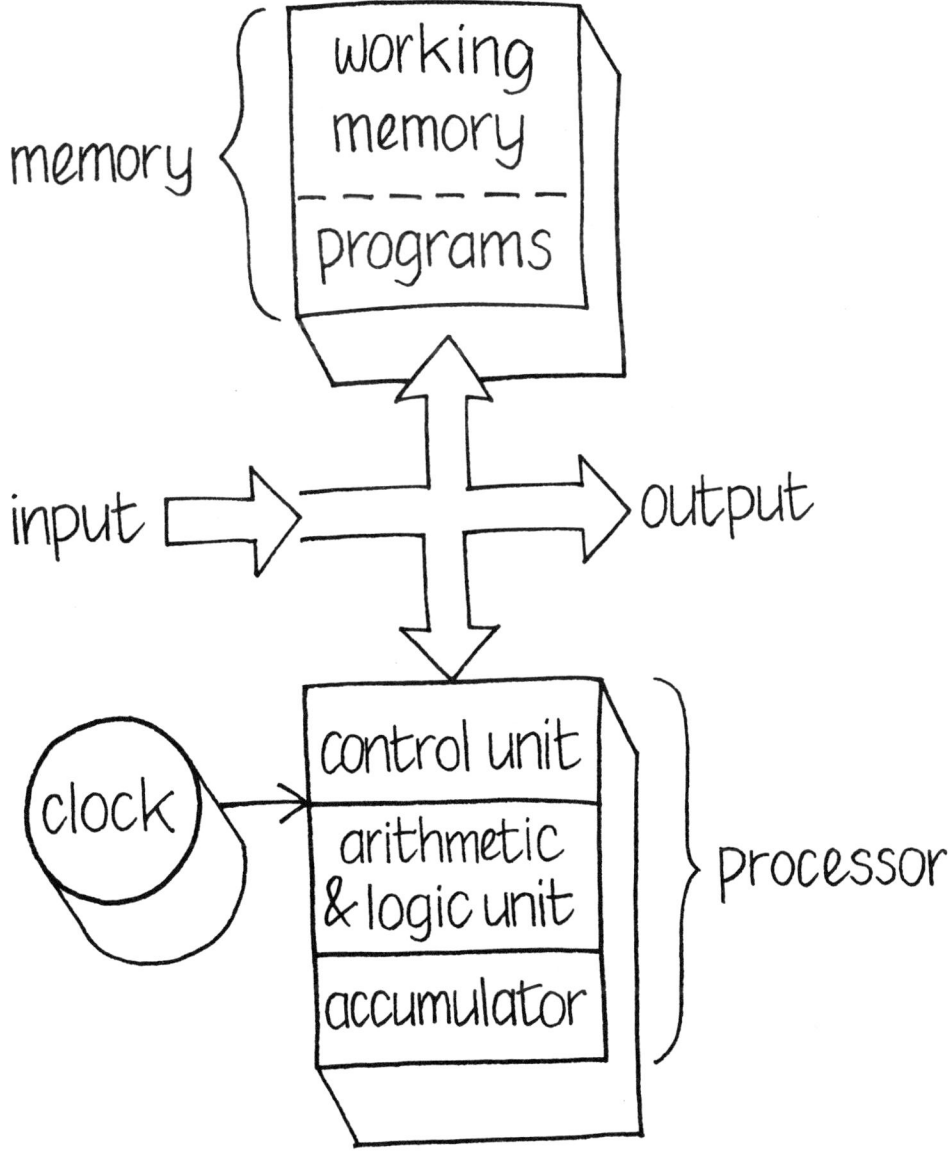

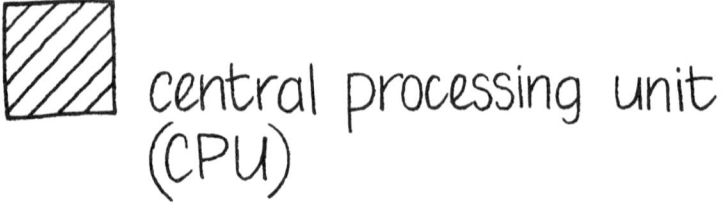central processing unit (CPU)

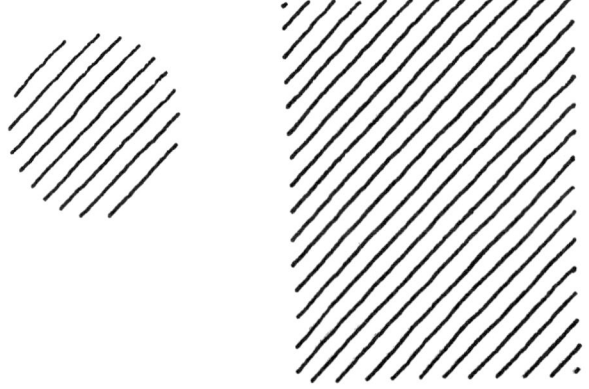

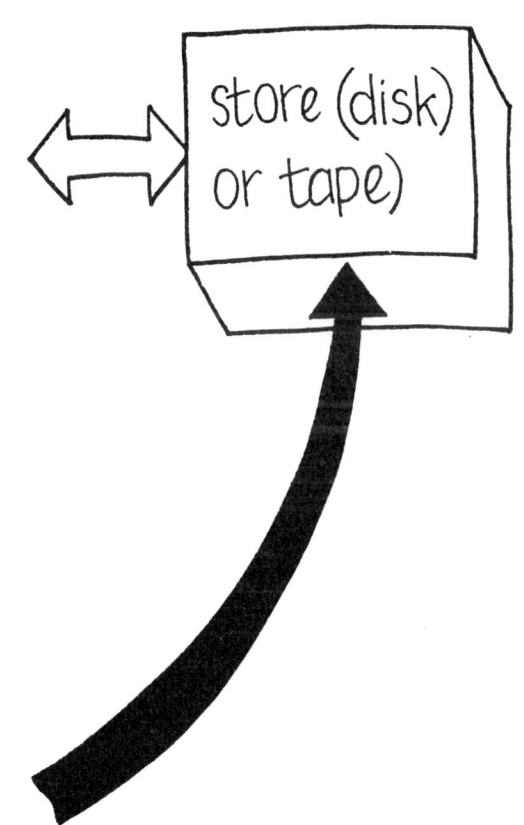

Three Categories of Systems Software

- Operating system

- Utilities

- Compilers, assemblers, interpreters

This is the software which supervises the running of applications programs and controls the operations of the various input/output devices, e.g. keyboard, VDU, printer, etc.

Purpose of an Operating System:

to provide a standard interface between an applications program and the hardware . . . hence the (theoretical) **portability of software**

Software

— a generic term for **programs**

A specific piece of software may comprise a number of linked programs

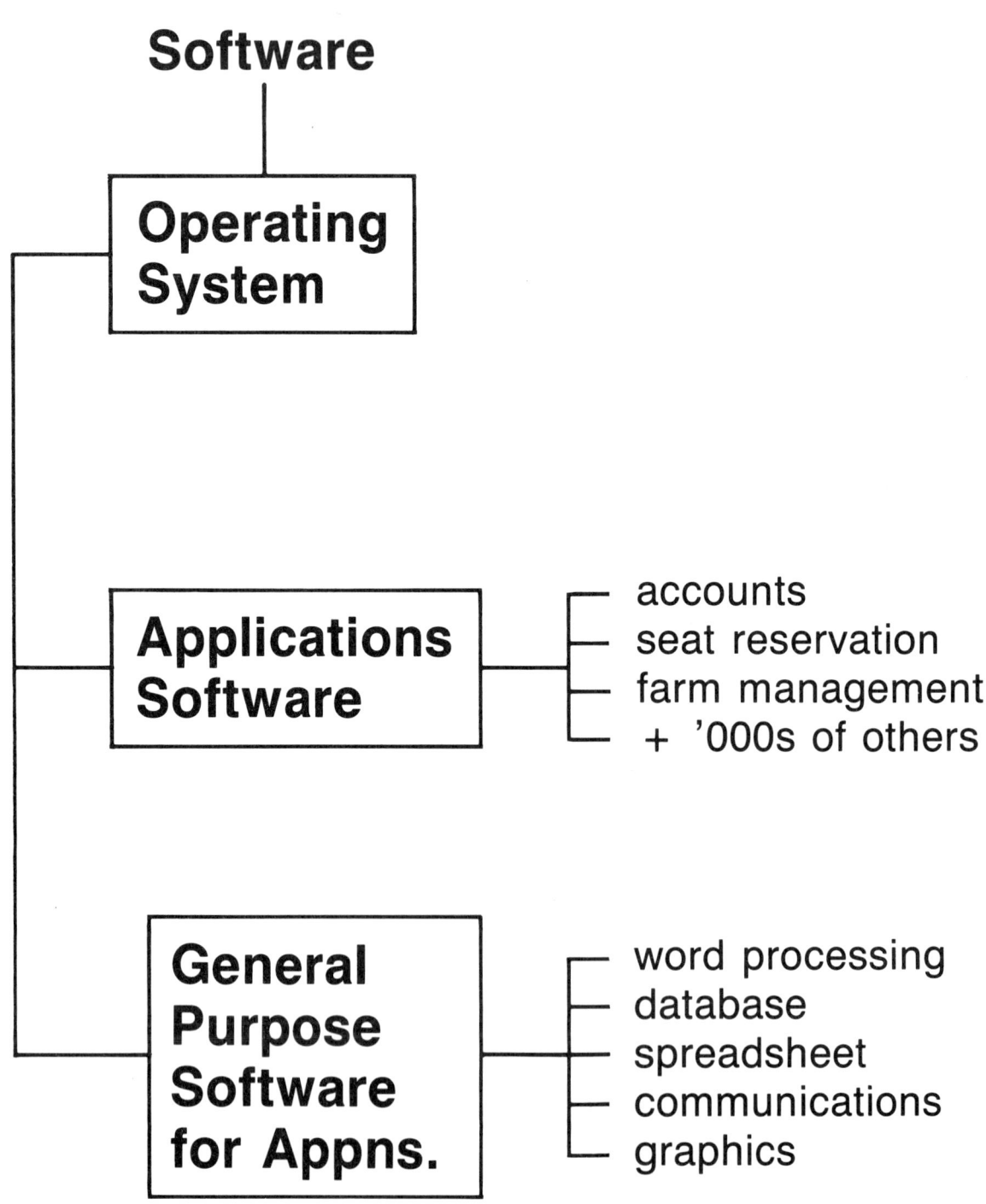

File Names & File Organization

File names may include letters or numbers and may be up to eight characters in length.

File names must not include spaces or characters (e.g. full stops) which have specific significance to the computer operating system software.

File names may have an 'extension' of up to 3 characters. Some extensions have specific significance
e.g.

    .COM a command file
    .EXE a relocatable executable file
    .DAT a data file
    .BAT a batch file
    .BAK a back-up file

A disk may be organized into multi-level sub-directories, thus simulating files within drawers, within filing cabinets.

Operating System Structure

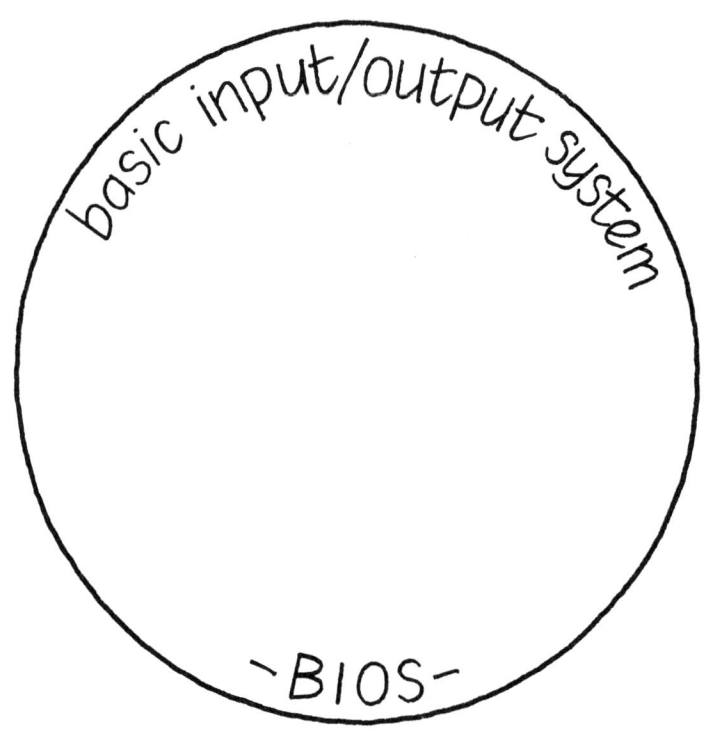

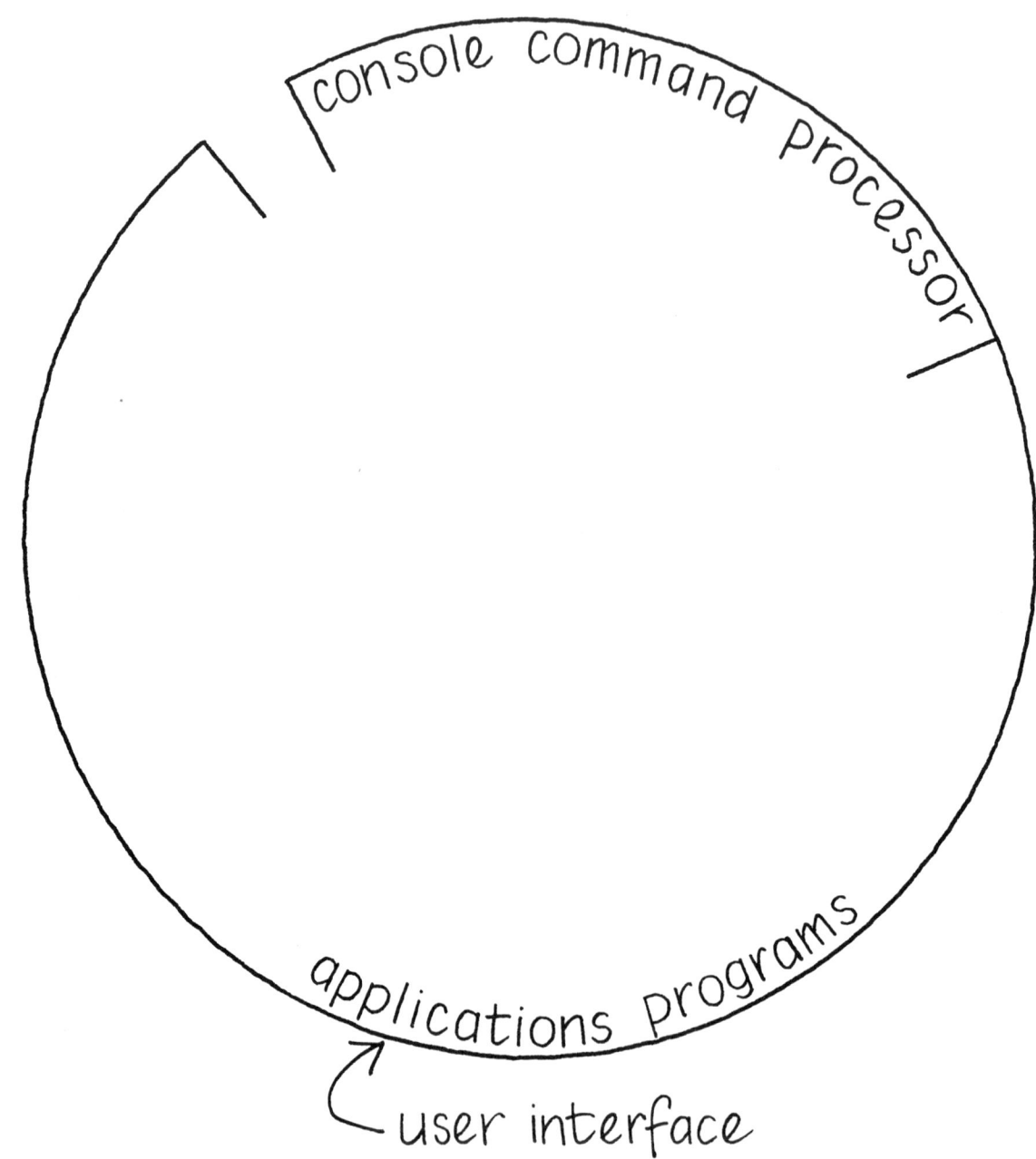

The Console Command Processor

This interprets and executes commands typed in at the keyboard – usually not directly, but by loading and running a command program **(.COM)** to do the job.

That program is in control of the system whilst running; afterwards control returns to the CCP, i.e. the program COMMAND.COM.

The CCP handles all input/output through the BDOS layer.

Main Functions of an Operating System

- Supervision of all operations within the computer including execution of programs
- Allocation of memory
- Control of input/output operations
- Handling of error conditions and recovery from them
- Provision of a range of 'internal' commands
- On a multi-user system, the logging of operations and charging of costs to user departments
- Provision of a standard interface between applications software and the hardware

System Commands

Internal

provided by operating system software which is resident in memory after the system has been 'booted'

(they are held in the file COMMAND.COM)

External

require the appropriate utility command program to be run

(implication: it must be available on the disk in the logged drive)

Illustration of Check Digit Computation

Consider a 6-figure stock item code which does not include a check digit
   e.g. 458612

Stage 1: multiply successive digits by 1, 2, 3, etc.

Stage 2: add the products and divide the result by 11, so as to produce an integral quotient & remainder

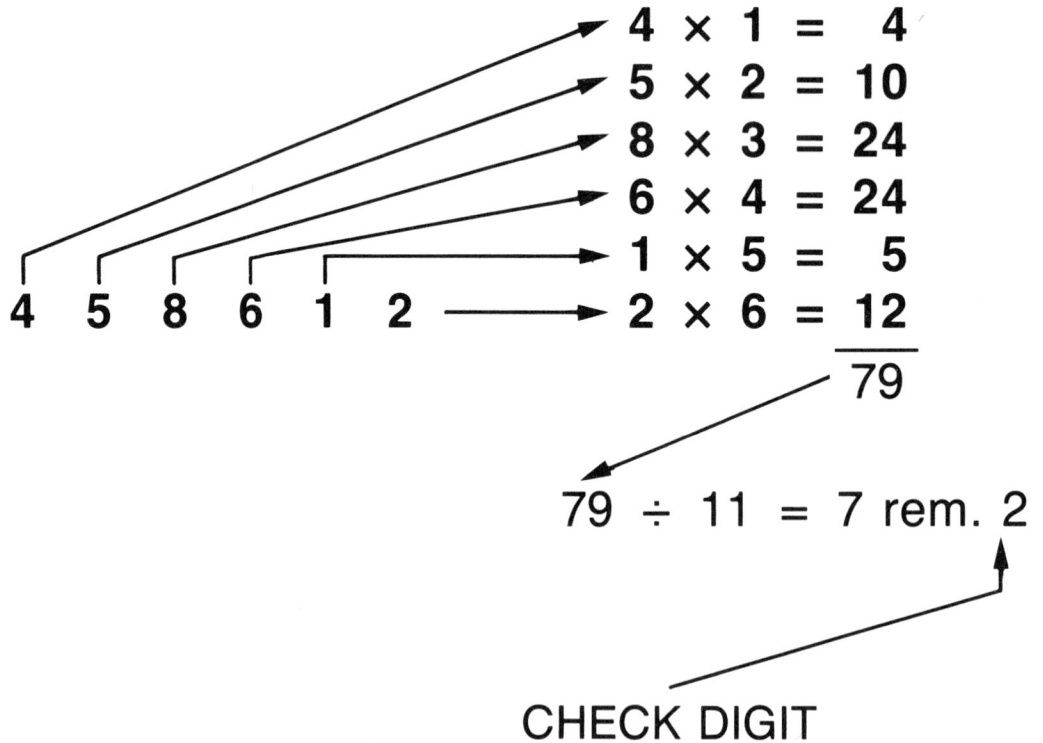

THE NEW STOCK ITEM CODE BECOMES 4586122

Appendix 2

I ASCII character codes

Dec	Hex	CHR	Dec	Hex	CHR	Dec	Hex	CHR
000	00H	NUL	043	2BH	+	086	56H	V
001	01H	SOH	044	2CH	,	087	57H	W
002	02H	STX	045	2DH	-	088	58H	X
003	03H	ETX	046	2EH	.	089	59H	Y
004	04H	EOT	047	2FH	/	090	5AH	Z
005	05H	ENQ	048	30H	0	091	5BH	[
006	06H	ACK	049	31H	1	092	5CH	\
007	07H	BEL	050	32H	2	093	5DH	]
008	08H	BS	051	33H	3	094	5EH	^
009	09H	HT	052	34H	4	095	5FH	_
010	0AH	LF	053	35H	5	096	60H	'
011	0BH	VT	054	36H	6	097	61H	a
012	0CH	FF	055	37H	7	098	62H	b
013	0DH	CR	056	38H	8	099	63H	c
014	0EH	SO	057	39H	9	100	64H	d
015	0FH	SI	058	3AH	:	101	65H	e
016	10H	DLE	059	3BH	;	102	66H	f
017	11H	DC1	060	3CH	<	103	67H	g
018	12H	DC2	061	3DH	=	104	68H	h
019	13H	DC3	062	3EH	>	105	69H	i
020	14H	DC4	063	3FH	?	106	6AH	j
021	15H	NAK	064	40H	@	107	6BH	k
022	16H	SYN	065	41H	A	108	6CH	l
023	17H	ETB	066	42H	B	109	6DH	m
024	18H	CAN	067	43H	C	110	6EH	n
025	19H	EM	068	44H	D	111	6FH	o
026	1AH	SUB	069	45H	E	112	70H	p
027	1BH	ESCAPE	070	46H	F	113	71H	q
028	1CH	FS	071	47H	G	114	72H	r
029	1DH	GS	072	48H	H	115	73H	s
030	1EH	RS	073	49H	I	116	74H	t
031	1FH	US	074	4AH	J	117	75H	u
032	20H	SPACE	075	4BH	K	118	76H	v
033	21H	!	076	4CH	L	119	77H	w
034	22H	"	077	4DH	M	120	78H	x
035	23H	#	078	4EH	N	121	79H	y
036	24H	$	079	4FH	O	122	7AH	z
037	25H	%	080	50H	P	123	7BH	{
038	26H	&	081	51H	Q	124	7CH		
039	27H	'	082	52H	R	025	7DH	}
040	28H	(	083	53H	S	126	7EH	~
041	29H	)	084	54H	T	127	7FH	DEL
042	2AH	*	085	55H	U			

Dec = decimal, Hex = hexadecimal (H), CHR = character, LF = Line Feed, FF = Form Feed, CR = Carriage Return, DEL = Rubout

II Word processing exercise 1

The following passage contains information about the Health &
Safety at Work Act (1974) which you need to know.

It also contains typing errors. Read the passage first for
interest and then check for:

1   Spelling
2   Format
3   Headings

                The Health & Safety at Work Act (1974)

Who is responsible?

From a legal standpoint, the principle responsability for
insuring the health and safety of peopel at work rests with
there employer.

At the same time, workers, too, have legal duties to
co-operate with the employer in meeting health and safty
requirements, for example, and not to interfere or misuse
anything provided in the interests of health and safety.

Responsibility for enforcing health and safety standard in the
workplaces rests with health and safety inspectos. In many
cases, these inspectors will be officers of the Health and
Safety Executive. However, the enforcing authority for some
premises - mostly offices, shops, warehouse, restaurants and
hotels - are local authorities whose H&S inspecters work in the
councils environmental health department.

If there is something wrong inyour workplace
If you think there is anything that is unsafe in your workplace,
first of all mention it to your supervisor, Always make your
point politely. Put your point over in the form of a question.
For example:

    "Do you think we could make that cabling under the desks
    any safer."

It is better if you can also make a positive suggestion about
improvement:

    "Do you think if we rearranged the desks like this .... it
    would make that loose cabling less of a risk?"

NEVER demand that something be done about it now, or else! For
instance, if you said:

    I think it is downright disgusting the conditions we have
    to work in. No one cares. Just look ar those cables on
    the floor over there. You could break your ****** neck."

If your supervisor does nothing about it after while, raise the question again - POLITELY. If still nothing is done about it, check that youre colleagues feel the same way. Then raise the mater with some a bit more senior. Or, consult a trade union or staff association representitive, if there is one.

If nothing is done about the problem then your only cause of action is to consult your local authoritys Environmental Health Department. They will ask your employer firmly to put things right.

What about your responsability?

Dont forget that you too have a responsibility not to create hazards or act in a way that could cause injury to others. The basic rules are:

1   Do not rush around the office

2   Be tidy - do not leave your bags or belongings where someone could fall over them

3   Use any protective clothing or equipment provided. You may think you look silly wearing goggles or rubber gloves, but if a spark flew into your eye, or if a dangerous substance burnt away all your skin, you'd look even sillier.

Be warned

If someone is injured at work, the person responsible for the accident will be prosecuted under law. That could be your employer ... but it could be you.

III Word processing exercise 2

First read the following passage for interest - it will help you to write good curriculum vitae.

Then read it again. Check:

i) Spelling
ii) Format
iii) Headings - are they in a sensible style and hierarchy?

How proper CV can top the pile

When an atractive job is advertised it is common for recruiters to get well over 100 relies. One firm of leading accountants reports getting around 2,000 from and ad. in the sunday times. Responses like that mean that someone had to wade through hundreds of pages of CVs. Inevitably their have to be some rapid judgements about who is worth interviewing.

So what will catch the recruiters eye?

a) Applications that are clealy set out, where the salient points relevent to the job in question can be eazily spotted.

Read the advertisement carefully, becase the advert is telling you what the recruiter is looking for and so the whole weight of the reply should focus on it.

CVs produced in bulk as part of a personal marketing campaign are easily spotted and suggest that the candidate is on the lookout, rather than making a planned career change.

Employers like to see evidence that you have given a good deal of thought to the way your experience matches their needs.

What if you don't exactly meet the specificatoin?

Very few people ever do - don't worry. What the advert says represents the recruiters ideal. It is a question of using your judgement, but there are some rules of thumb to observe.

a) When an advert calls for applications from people aged around 30, this means that people between 28 and 37 will be considered. A similar principal applies to qualifications and experience.

b) The question of experience. If a job calls for a degree and five years' experience, a recruiter wouldn't look at someone with only O leverls. But it that person had, say, eight years' experience with a good company that had a reputation for providing top-notch training, he or she would certainly go on the list of possibilities.,

How much am I worth?

How does it look if you apply for a job but the salary offered is far greater than the one your currently have? How does it look if you apply for a job where the salary is the same as your current one?

Employers aren't too worried by about candidates looking for a big increase if their CV suggests they are underpaid but well qualified.

The latter looks like a sideways more - and that could be a mistake. Your letter of application would have to explain cleraly why your reasons sor such a move.

The impression is important

It is a question of the totality of an impresion. A recruiter expects candidates to fill not less than 50% of the requirements. The view he takes of the area where the fit is incomplete will depend on the covering letter.

Read the advertisement carefully - the advert is the key to it all.

It can sometimes - unintentionally - tell you more about the job that the bare essentials of what it entails. If it is vague on any point, that in itself is revealing.

Advertisements that talk of exciting but unspecified opportunities or that dangle telephone-number salaries without stating what you have to do for them are often the rougher end of commission selling.

More precisoly worded texts can alsow ring warning bells. Terms such as "dynamice" or "fast-growing" can be euphemisms for "hire and fire". "Self-motivating" ofetn means that you will be given an target ad led to get on with it, without much guidance.

Watch our for the adverts that are stiff with management jargon - they carry the hidden message that unless you can talk the same jargon you wont fit.

Before you even get to the interview, you may be subject to the recruiter's personal prejudices, but there is not much you can do about that. You can however, mak sure hat your letter and CV are well presented. Use good quality paper envelopes and make sure they are free of any spelling errors.

Remember, if you are not called for interview there may be a good reason. There may also be so many applications for the job that there are simply better candidates than you around at the time. However, that does not mean that you are not any good. Just keep trying.

IV Conversion grid for calculating line and character positions

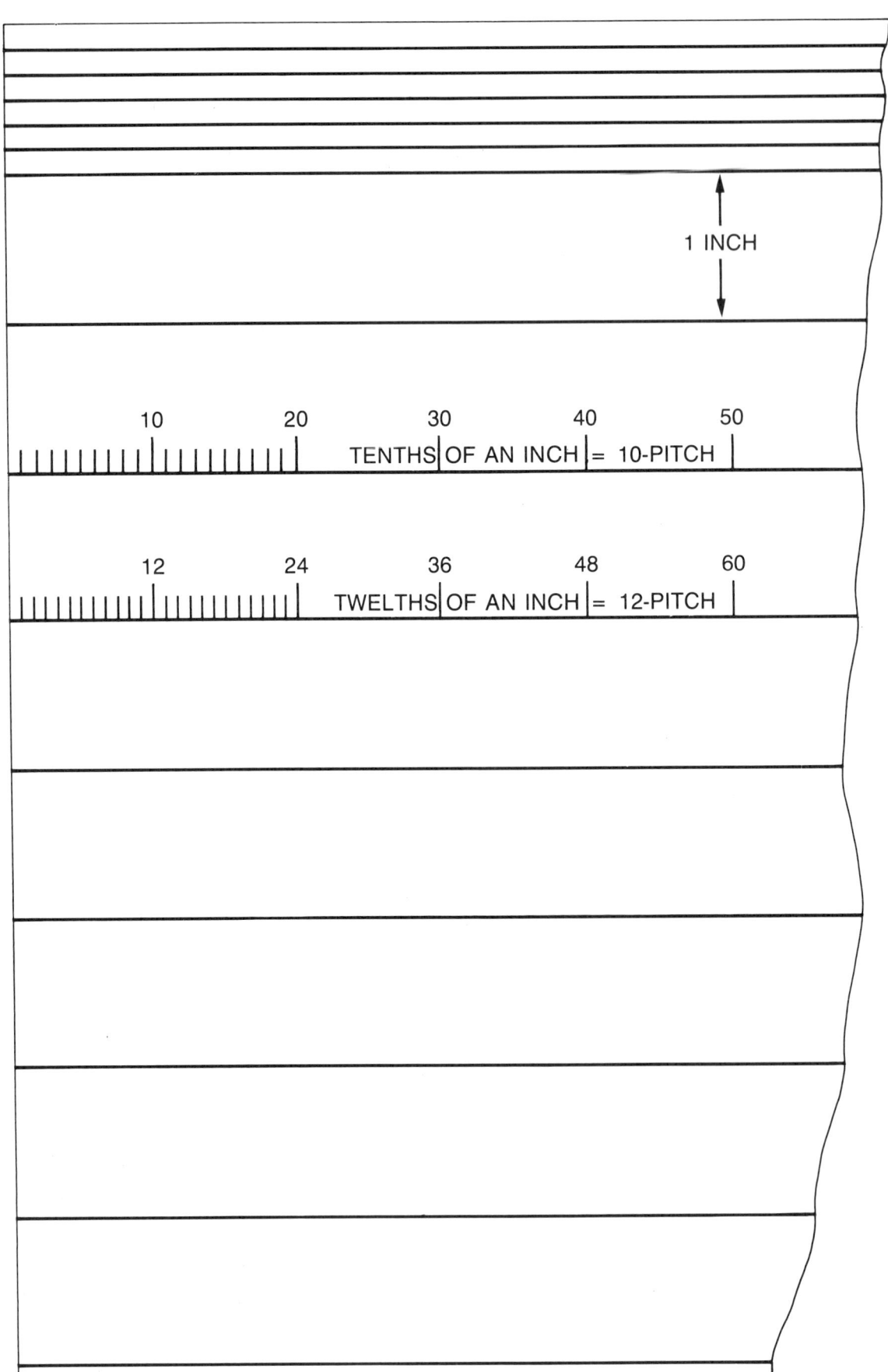

V P11 tax form

Deductions working sheet P11 (New)

208

Employer's name		Employee's surname in CAPITAL LETTERS	First two forenames		Tax Code †	Amended code †	Year to 5 April
							19......
Tax District and reference		National Insurance no.	Date of birth in figures Day | Month | Year	Date of leaving in figures Day | Month | Year		Week/Month/ no. in which applied	

National Insurance Contributions

Total of Employee's and Employer's Contributions payable 1a	Employee's contributions payable 1b	Employee's contributions at Contracted-out rate included in Col. 1b 1c	Statutory sick pay in the week or month included in col. 2 1d	MONTH number	WEEK number	Pay in the week or month including statutory sick pay 2	Works no. etc. Total pay to date 3	PAYE Income Tax Total free pay to date as shown by Table A 4	Total taxable pay to date 5	Total tax due to date as shown by Taxable Pay ables 6	Tax deducted or refunded in the week or month Mark refunds "R" 7	For employer's use
£	£	£	£			£	£	£	£	£	£	
Bt. fwd.	Bt. fwd.	Bt. fwd.	Bt. fwd.	B.F. from Mth. 7	B.F. from Wk. 30		Bt. fwd.			Bt. fwd.		
					31							
				6 Nov. to 5 Dec.	32							
					33							
					34							
				8	35							
				6 Dec. to 5 Jan.	36							
					37							
					38							
				9	39							
				6 Jan. to 5 Feb.	40							
					41							
					42							
				10	43							
				6 Feb. to 5 Mar.	44							
					45							
					46							
				11	47							
				6 Mar. to 5 April	48							
					49							
					50							
					51							
				12	52							
					§							

▼ STATUTORY SICK PAY TOTAL

▼ PAY AND TAX TOTALS:
Previous employments
This employment
Mark net refund "R"

N.I. Cont'n Table Letter ▶

‡ **N.I. LETTER:** Enter letter identifying contribution table used when making first entry on sheet and on any subsequent change of table.

N.I. TOTALS: Enter in columns 1a, 1b and 1c separate contribution TOTALS for each table used.

† *If amended cross out previous code*

§ *Complete this line if pay day falls on 5 April (in leap years 4 & 5 April). See Week 53 instructions in the Employer's Guide to PAYE.*

Employee's Widows & Orphans /Life insurance contributions in this employment £

Printed in UK for HMSO D8400967 10 84 38369

P11 (New) *Keep this form for not less than 3 years after the end of the year to which it relates, or longer if directed.*